ISAAC AND JACOB,
GOD'S CHOSEN ONES

This is VOLUME TWO of
THE BIBLE IN HISTORY
A Contemporary Companion to the Bible

Edited by Father Robert Tamisier, P.S.S.
*Advisory Editor for the English
Language Edition:* Joseph Rhymer
Editorial Consultants:
Father Edward J. Ciuba
Bishop John J. Dougherty
Rabbi Samuel Sandmel
Dr Samuel L. Terrien

Isaac and Jacob, God's Chosen Ones

by HENRI GAUBERT

Translated by Lancelot Sheppard

A Giniger Book
published in association with
HASTINGS HOUSE, PUBLISHERS
NEW YORK

CONTENTS

PREFACE

The Bible is a single book in which the pattern of God's work in his world can be traced through two thousand years of human history. There is a single pattern running through it all, and fundamentally it is a simple pattern. The complexity comes from the complexity of human history.

But the Bible is also a collection of books. Some of them grew out of folk tales, and stories from the nation's past, which were handed down from father to son, or told round the pilgrims' camp fires at the places where the people went to worship. Some of the books were written by men who can be named and placed in their historical situation, and some are anonymous and can only be given a firm date with difficulty. The whole collection grew slowly over many centuries, and was repeatedly edited and rearranged, until it reached the form in which we now have it.

This means that the Bible has never been a book which could be read without help. Even in New Testament times, people found parts of it obscure. Customs which are taken for granted, and ways of life which are accepted without question by people who have never known anything different, may be strange to the later reader and difficult to understand. This is more than ever true in our own times, when the society in which we live has changed so much, even during the last hundred years.

This present series of books is for use as a Companion to the Bible. They are not a substitute for the Bible, for nothing can take the place of the Bible itself. It impresses itself on those who read it seriously in a way that no other book can. Some of the difficulties about reading the Bible have been due to the way in which it has usually been printed. Many of these are overcome in the Jerusalem Bible, a translation in contemporary English which is used in this series. In the Jerusalem Bible the text is presented by dividing the books into sections, and providing headings and footnotes.

The aim of this present series of books is to help people to understand the divine revelation. It presents the Bible in the historical circumstances in which it developed. The men and women who were so acutely aware of God's active presence in their lives were all people of their times. Their experiences were the same as the experiences of their neighbours and fellow-countrymen. They earned their living by the same skills and trades, and their thoughts were expressed in the language used by everyone around them. To understand how God was revealing himself to these people, we must share their experiences as far as we can, and know what was happening in the world in which they lived.

Using the findings of archaeology and of historical research, the books in this series show the circumstances and the environment in which God made himself known. During recent years great advances have been made in our knowledge of the Near East during the period when the Bible was written, but these advances have only been possible because of the foundations laid patiently by scholars for more than a hundred years.

This series of books does not attempt to record all of the most recent finds, for new discoveries often have to be examined with caution before there can be certainty about their significance. Only those views which are accepted by a wide range of scholars are used here. It is impressive and reassuring to see how far the discoveries of the archaeologists and historians have confirmed the authenticity of details given in the Bible. Again and again, objects have been discovered, and sites have been excavated, which have confirmed the picture given by the Bible itself. There are many hindrances to archaeological work in the Near East. Political frontiers are often real barriers, and many important sites are still centres of worship where a thorough investigation is not possible. But we can be confident that new discoveries, as they are confirmed and analysed, will deepen our understanding of the times when the foundations of our religion were laid.

It is sometimes thought that books such as these should attempt to give the historical background to the Bible without any mention of God. This is impossible. The Bible is history, but it is also sacred history. It is history viewed and written with the knowledge that God is the active source of all history, and that all events are part of the movement towards the final consummation which God has willed. There is a pattern in the events of history, and God shows himself through this pattern. The events will not make sense, nor will they be worth studying, unless we see them from the point of view of the people who found God in them. We cannot make sense of the events if we leave God out.

The modern reader is sometimes surprised by the strange ways in which ancient historians presented their material, but much of this strangeness comes from the way in which ancient authors set about their task. Many of the writers of the Bible felt that their main responsibility was to preserve the traditions and the accounts of the events with as little alteration as possible. They were 'scribes' rather than authors. They copied out whatever information they could find, or selected the best descriptions and the parts that they thought mattered most. Then they stitched the pieces together without changing the words or the style.

They collected their information wherever they could find it, so their work contains poetry, epics, fiction, official chronicles, anecdotes, family and tribal memoirs, royal decrees, codes of law, letters, rules for priests. These, and many others, are the kind of sources which historians use in any age; they are the raw material of history, and without them the historian would be helpless. But in the ancient historian's writings this raw material has a marked effect on the way in which the history is written. There is much repetition and, sometimes, contradiction, when the 'author' uses two versions of the same event. But there is also a vivid immediacy about it all which helps us to come close to the people who took part in the event and to appreciate the effect it had upon them.

The account is presented to us in the people's own words, so we find that we can share more easily in their experiences, and appreciate more easily their point of view. It is the point of view of a people who recognised God's active presence, and who responded to his presence with worship.

Occasionally we can detect a further motive which has shaped some of the books of the Bible. The biblical writers were never mere historians. They only wrote about the past if it could throw light on their present situation. They wanted to show how God had acted in the past, so that the people of their own times could see God's presence and power at work in their own lives. So the biblical historians selected from the material available, and then arranged it so that the lessons were as obvious as it was possible to make them.

When we read these passages we are seeing the events of history through the eyes of men who frequently were writing about those events many generations after they had occurred. The books they wrote were expressions of the faith of the men who wrote them, and they were written to strengthen the faith of the people who read them. They have more to say about that faith than they have about the historical details of the events on which that faith was built.

Sometimes the books of the Bible contain deliberate anachronisms. This can be seen, for example, in some of the words and actions attributed to Moses. Moses had a greater influence on the Hebrew people than any other man. Later, in times of urgent need or of national reform, it was only natural for men to ask themselves what Moses would have done if he had been faced with their problems. The action taken, or the programme of reform, was then recorded as if Moses himself had foreseen the situation and had legislated for it. This is why so much of the law is written as if it had been given by Moses.

The men who wrote in this way were expressing an important truth. Whenever the nation was unfaithful to God, it was because it had forgotten the principles which Moses had taught to his generation of Hebrews. Those principles lay at the heart of the Hebrew faith, but the people of each new generation had to apply them to the changing circumstances of their times. The convention of making Moses the author of all their laws was the clearest way of showing that those laws were expressions of the central traditions of the nation.

The people of the Bible recognised the thread of God's revelation in the ordinary events of their lives. This series of books shows what those events were, and how that thread fits into its historical background. Each book may be read on its own, but the books are also linked together to form a continuous exposition and elucidation of the way in which God has made himself known through the Bible. The titles in the series are:

Each book contains the necessary maps, diagrams and illustrations for the period with which it is concerned. The reader is also recommended to use the chronological table, the maps and the general information printed after the New Testament in the Jerusalem Bible Standard Edition.

Joseph Rhymer,
Editor of the English Language Edition.

1

ISAAC: THE NEW CHIEFTAIN OF THE HEBREW CLAN

Then Abraham breathed his last, dying at a ripe old age, an old man who had lived his full span of years; and he was gathered to his people. . . . After Abraham's death God blessed his son Isaac, and Isaac lived near the well of Lahai Roi (Gen. 25: 7, 11).

The date was about 1800 B.C. In the oak-grove of Mamre, near the city of Hebron, the shepherds' camp was in mourning. In the black tent of woven goats' hair, Abraham, the old nomad chieftain, the Aramean patriarch, the one 'loved by God', as the Bible calls him, had just breathed his last. In noisy and somewhat ostentatious fashion the assembled company gave vent to their grief.

Abraham *was gathered to his people* says Genesis on this occasion. Sometimes, in speaking of a dead person, he was described as having 'gone down into Sheol', the term used to designate the underground dwelling of the departed. In this dark, desolate place the 'shade', although not entirely devoid of feelings, continued to lead a rather sad and diminished existence. During the period which concerns us the Hebrews had no idea of a moral reward after death.

Abraham's body was taken to the funeral cave of Machpelah which had recently been fitted out as a

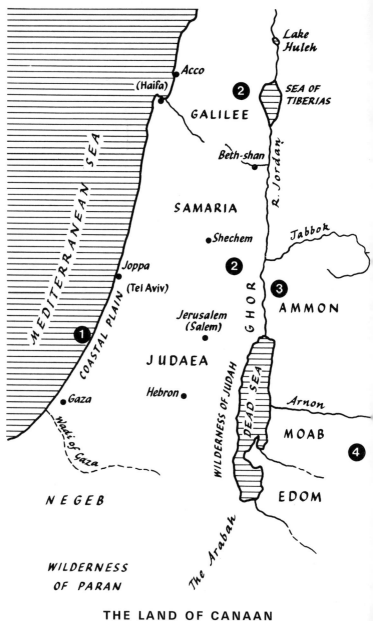

THE LAND OF CANAAN
Ancient Palestine

Smallness of the Land of Canaan.

It is quite a small country amounting to a little less than 10,000 square miles (if the territory east of the Jordan is included), smaller therefore than the State of Maryland in the U.S.A. and only a little larger than Wales in the U.K.

The four natural regions of the Land of Canaan.

There are four principal natural regions, dividing the country into parallel strips:

1. The coastal plain of the Mediterranean from the Wadi of Gaza (the modern Ghazzeh) to the last spur of the Camel range.

2. Between the Mediterranean and the Jordan: the hills of Galilee (to the north) which after the gap made by the plain of Jezreel (or Esdraelon) continue to the south by the mountain masses of Samaria (or Mount Ephraim) and of Judaea.

3. The Ghor or valley of the Jordan.

4. To the east of the Jordan, between and the Arabian Desert the mountain mass of Bajan, Gilead, Moab (in general the mountains and steppes of the modern kingdom of Jordan).

1. The coastal plain

From Mount Carmel to the Wadi of Gaza is the low coastal region, rectilinear in shape (save for the Carmel spur). Along the whole line of coast is a fringe of sand dunes. To the east of these dunes a plain of rich soil brought down by the streams forms the richest region of Palestine. The climate is mild, the soil fertile, and there is enough water. As the east is approached the plain becomes increasingly drier. This is the corn-growing region and is also suitable for cattle rearing. The richness of the soil here forms a strange contrast with the poverty of adjoining Judaea.

2. In the north is Galilee, the land of hills, springs and forests. This pleasant region is formed by the two mountain masses with the fertile plain of Jezreel (or Esdraelon) in between.

To the south of the plain of Jezreel is the massif of Samaria (with Shechem). Undulating country with abundant springs and rich pasture land.

To the south of the massif of Samaria is that of Judaea. The plateau stretches from the Hebron to Jerusalem; there are highlands with a harsh winter climate and few springs or streams, but wells have been dug almost everywhere. Little or no forest land occurs and cultivation is difficult. There are steppes on which flocks of sheep or goats can find food.

In the west between Judaea and the Mediterranean the Shephala lies the corn-growing district with abundant water.

To the east of the Jordan, the wilderness of Judaea (or Judah) slopes down to the Dead Sea.

To the south of Judaea is the Negeb, a dry, desert region.

3. The Ghor ('hole' or 'hollow').

This is the long rift valley stretching from the Lake of Tiberias to the Dead Sea. Its lowest point occurs where it enters the Dead Sea, 1,290 feet below the level of the Mediterranean. The Ghor is a desert through which the Jordan flows; but in the narrow alluvial plain there is plentiful vegetation.

4. The plateaux of the East (Transjordania).

To the east of the Ghor, dominating the rift from a height of 4,000 feet, a high plateau rises abruptly which then slopes down to the eastern desert. We can here distinguish the three principal regions mentioned by the Bible:

To the north the land of Gilead, not unlike Judaea.

In the centre, Moab, which is fairly fertile.

In the south Edom, almost a desert.

family vault by Abraham himself. Behind the procession of weeping mourners walked Ishmael and Isaac, the two sons of the dead man. On a stone shelf, similar to that on which lay the remains of Sarah, the ancestress, were placed the mortal remains of Abraham, wrapped up in a sheepskin unless, following the Sumerian custom, a reed mat was used. In any case, there was no embalming such as the Egyptians did. Beside the corpse bowls were placed and a jar full of water. Then the heavy boulder was rolled back into place to secure the entrance, which at this period was usually a cleft in the rock.

A legal question: was Ishmael Abraham's heir?

During the funeral ceremony at Machpelah all present seemed to regard Isaac as the only heir of the dead patriarch. And yet the firstborn of the family was not, as it happened, Isaac but Ishmael. It cannot be argued that Ishmael was the son of a concubine and that the law barred him from the inheritance. In fact at his birth Ishmael was formally recognized as a legitimate child. The facts were these: Sarah, Abraham's wife, grieved at her prolonged sterility. On the subject of adoption she could avail herself of a provision of the ancient Babylonian laws to which the Hebrew clan, natives of the delta of the Euphrates, for long remained faithful. According to this, a wife who did not succeed in producing a child could choose one of her slaves 'to take into' her husband and if, as a result, this slave girl gave birth 'on the lap' of the legal wife, the child would henceforth be considered as the wife's own child; in law he would possess all the prerogatives of a legitimate child. Now that is what had happened: Sarah gave Abraham her Egyptian slave Hagar who gave birth 'on Sarah's lap' to Ishmael. Everything thus seemed for the best.

On the other hand, we know that some fifteen years

4

later, and contrary to all expectation, Sarah gave birth to Isaac. She then started a harsh campaign against Hagar the concubine and her son Ishmael, telling Abraham continually that the son of the slave girl must on no account share the inheritance with her own son Isaac. Sarah was successful and the concubine and her son were driven out into the wilderness. They managed to settle in the wilderness of Paran, a desolate and hostile region forming part of the Sinai massif. It is now conceded that Abraham ought not to have abandoned them completely.

It remains true, nonetheless, that in accordance with Sumerian law in force among these wandering shepherds, Ishmael ought to have been regarded not only as a legitimate son (because he was legally adopted) but also as the possessor of all the rights of the elder son, and thereby entitled to a greater share than his brother in the inheritance. In addition, as a general rule the firstborn was regarded as the father's spiritual heir and as the future head of the family. In these circumstances how can it be explained that at Abraham's death we find Isaac taking possession of the inheritance and assuming the leadership of the clan?

A spiritual question: Isaac as Abraham's sole heir

Obviously it was no function of Sumerian law to regulate or indeed to hinder the plans of Yahweh. If he chose as confidant and collaborator an obscure Aramean shepherd it was because the small Hebrew clan under the leadership of Abraham was better suited than others to receive the spiritual responsibilities.

Yahweh revealed his plans to Abraham: 'It is through Isaac that your name shall be carried on.' In other words, the line of the patriarchs would descend from Isaac and not from Ishmael. Of course, Ishmael remained under divine protection: he was to be the ancestor of a great nation: his twelve sons were to become the chieftains of the twelve tribes of Ishmaelite Arabs of north Arabia. But the torch of revelation was to be jealously retained in the hands of the descendants of Abraham and Isaac alone.

For it was a question of protecting the Hebrew clan against any intrusion of elements of polytheism. Ishmael, the son of Hagar the Egyptian, was of mixed blood; his religious heritage was probably of a popular nature, namely, the crude mixture of god-beasts and beast-gods worshipped on the banks of the Nile. How, in such circumstances could he be chosen as the guardian of the new Hebrew faith governed by the one, holy and invisible God?

After his father's funeral Ishmael could well have spoken out to claim his rightful share of the inheritance. But he probably understood that despite the provisions of the Sumerian law he had remained in the eyes of the Hebrew clan the 'concubine's son', the 'slave girl's child'. He could sense that his position was by no means assured. He appeared at the funeral, and then, without a word, he went back to his tents.

Moreover, to show clearly the complete rupture between Ishmael and the Hebrew clan the writer of Genesis takes care to tell us that, in the wilderness of Paran, Ishmael, who had become a mighty hunter and a clever hand with a bow and arrow, founded a family. His mother, Hagar the Egyptian, chose him an Egyptian woman for wife. Thus there was a twofold admixture of blood. At the historical level, which coincides here with the religious, the son of Hagar the slave is no longer important.

Ishmael and Mohammed

The Bible hardly mentions Ishmael again, but the Koran

dwellers, were engulfed in the most barbarous practices returns to the question and makes it a polemical one.

In the seventh century A.D., Mohammed, the caravaneer, the propagator of Islam, proclaiming himself to be the prophet of Allah, began to preach. At that period the inhabitants of Arabia, whether nomads or city dwellers, were engulfed in the most barbarous practices of polydemonism.

The monotheism of Islam is a theological notion taken from the Bible by Mohammed who, on his travels, had obtained knowledge of some passages from it. Relying on a few verses of Genesis which mention Ishmael, Mohammed adopted fairly and squarely the explanation furnished by the Old Testament. In his view Ishmael was the ancestor of the Arabs, Ishmael was the eldest son of Abraham and his heir. In legal fashion then, and appealing to the law of the desert, Mohammed claimed for the men of his race the material and spiritual inheritance of Abraham.

From this moment, war was declared between the sons of Isaac and those of Ishmael. Before Mohammed's time Jews and Arabs can scarcely be said to have been fond of each other. After the appearance of the Koran there was open hostility. The 'Arab question' came to the fore, particularly on the frontiers of the modern State of Israel.

At Abraham's funeral the patriarch's two sons, Ishmael and Isaac, met for the last time. It appeared necessary to make this digression in order to explain by means of the ancient texts a situation which is still tense at the present day.

Who was Isaac ?

The same question was asked about Abraham and the inquiry proved long and fairly complicated.

Isaac an historical character 'crushed' between his father Abraham and his son Jacob

In history it is by no means an advantage to be both the son of a man who has carried out a great plan and the father of a man of action. Isaac, the son of the brilliant Abraham and father of the dynamic Jacob appears to be crushed between these two sharply outstanding personalities. Although Abraham and Jacob were two very different characters they both set themselves energetically to carry out the plan which, in its principal features, God had revealed to them. These two patriarchs, both of them stout of heart and using methods in accordance with their own characters, threw themselves boldly into the struggle. No doubt there were occasional failures but the struggle was hard, long and heroic, nonetheless.

Isaac stands out far less clearly. According to the information furnished by the Bible he seems to have led a peaceful life as a nomad chieftain. He had no great anxieties and no difficult problems to solve. It is a rapid, almost offhand sketch with which the scribe has provided us; Isaac cannot be classed among those strong personalities who contrived to give a fresh impetus to events and to their own period.

Isaac's twofold character: the man and his mission

The Bible does not spare Isaac; in no way does it seek to give us an enhanced impression of him. Indeed it takes care not to pass over or minimize certain traits which emphasize the weakness of his character. Isaac was a typical oriental shepherd. He had an accurate knowledge of the course to be followed in going from pasture to pasture, and even contrived to improve it in its details. Over the tracks dotted with oases he ensured the necessary change of pasture for his flocks, and arranged very competently for the seasonal change of site for his camp. He managed to preserve, and even increase quite considerably, the numbers of the flocks and herds which he had inherited. He was a good administrator and an excellent chieftain of the clan.

On the other hand some of the episodes related in Genesis seem to show Isaac as of only medium intelligence, to say the least. Quite often his perspicacity is questionable; in the next chapter we shall see how easily he could be influenced by his entourage. It is all very well to insist on the fact that at that time Isaac was very old and almost blind, but it seems clear that the chieftain's authority had for some time past fallen into abeyance.

In addition, the details in our possession concerning Isaac both in youth and in maturity are at variance with his behaviour as an old man. Time and again he gives us the impression of being a man of weak character and indeed inconsistent. There is none of the superhuman greatness and the energetic, forceful activity evinced on occasion by Abraham. There is none of the subtlety, adroitness, and flexible diplomacy of Jacob.

Yet we must be careful not to be too severe in judging Isaac. No doubt at the human level he lacked the influential genius that we are perhaps too accustomed to discern in certain biblical characters. On the other hand it requires to be pointed out and indeed emphasized that in carrying out his spiritual mission Isaac always showed himself as a true son of Abraham. Moreover, Yahweh lost no time in confirming for Isaac and his people the idea of the one God. Among them there was no infiltration of the idolatrous Canaanite forms of worship which because of their proximity always formed a danger; nor was there any attempt to return to the ancient practices of their polytheistic ancestors.

Isaac had carried on the torch transmitted to him by his father; he was to pass it on, intact, to his descendants.

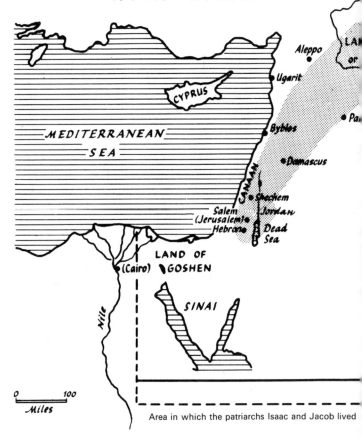

Only the western part of the Fertile Crescent, between Haran and the Delta (Land of Goshen).

Lake Van

Lake Urmia

Tigris

CASPIAN SEA

FATHERS
AHARAIIM

Ashur

•(Teheran)

Mari

A K K A D
•(Baghdad)

Euphrates

•Babylon

SUMER

Ur

PERSIAN GULF

in which the patriarch Abraham lived

Abraham came from Ur, halted at Haran, then went down by way of
Shechem, Bethel, Hebron (Mamre). There was a short period in Egypt.
In short the first Hebrew patriarch traversed the territory of the Fertile
Crescent from one end to the other.

And this spiritual role of Isaac's was by no means so easy as we in the twentieth century may be tempted to think.

To sum up: as a man Isaac appears to us as a somewhat vague character, but as a man with a mission, the bearer of the Revelation, he proved equal to his heavy task.

Isaac's life

A great part of Isaac's life has already been related in the story of Abraham: his birth foretold by Yahweh, the religious sacrifice commanded by Yahweh and halted at the very moment when Abraham raised the knife over the boy's body, the events preceding the choice of his wife and his marriage. These scenes, sometimes charming, at others dramatic, are in general agreement with the findings established by recent archaeological discoveries and the information provided by some of the Babylonian texts. Shortly we shall come to the chapter devoted to Jacob, called Israel. At this time Isaac was not yet dead so the last part of his life is incorporated in the extraordinary adventure of his son.

Between these two monumental historical narratives — the story of Abraham and the story of Jacob — the little that remains of the story of Isaac seems rather to be bathed in obscurity. But there can be no question, nevertheless, of passing over this part of biblical history in silence. It too requires a certain amount of explanation. What can be called Isaac's autonomous life can be divided as follows:

> confirmations of the Promise by Yahweh;
> some incidents of pastoral life.

The messages delivered to Isaac by Yahweh

In rapid outline the Bible relates the two successive appearances of Yahweh during which Isaac received

confirmations of the Promise, advice and encouragement. The first of these theophanies took place at Gerar,
the second at Beersheba.

Gerar,[1] the Bible informs us, was the capital city of
Abimelech, king of the Philistines.[2] On this occasion we
find Isaac leaving the usual pastoral circuit in the Negeb
for a time and making his way to the lowland or Shephelah. The reason for the move was the need for food – the
grass on the steppes was burned brown, the wells were
dry. To save both beasts and men it was urgently
necessary to find green pastures and oases. Between the
hill country of Judaea and the coastal plain with its rich
cereal crops there stretches a region of medium altitude
intersected with valleys in which good pastureland
abounds, a real dreamland for flocks almost dead with
hunger and thirst. Isaac knew the region; he was born
there at a time when Abraham too, under similar circumstances, was fleeing from the Negeb when it was burnt
brown by the sun.

In face of the persistent drought Isaac might well have
been tempted to turn towards the frontiers of the Nile
delta to 'ask for grass and water' from Pharaoh's officials.
There was a real danger that the small Hebrew clan who
were the guardians of the notion of the one God should
settle on the confines of Egyptian civilization which was
plunged in paganism strongly tinged with magic, with

[1] Archaeologists and biblical historians are divided on the precise locality of
this pastoral centre. It may well be that it is the Gerar marked on modern maps
and situated to the north-west of Beersheba. For the details of the controversy
see *La Genèse*, translated by R. de Vaux: O.P.—Genesis 20: 1, note b—W. F.
Albright, *The Archaeology of Palestine*, Penguin Books, Harmondsworth and
Baltimore, 1949, p. 39; M. Du Buit, O.P. and Raoul Blanchard, *The Geography
of the Holy Land*, Burns and Oates, London, 1966; American edn., *The Promised
Land*, Hawthorn, New York.

[2] This is an anachronism perpetrated by the writer of this chapter of Genesis.
At the period when he recorded this detail (sixth or fifth century B.C.) the
Philistines were occupying this region but they only established themselves in
this part of the land of Canaan in about 1200 B.C., that is, six centuries after the
time of Isaac. In reality, Abimelech was the chieftain of a Canaanite, that is, a
Semitic, tribe.

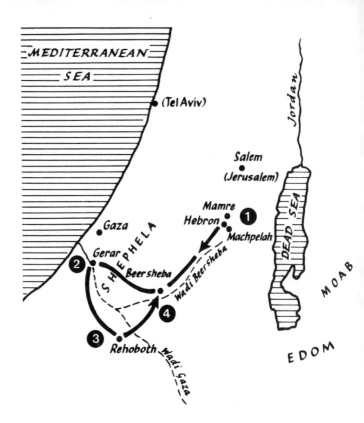

ISAAC'S JOURNEYS WITH HIS FLOCKS

1. The drought obliges Isaac to leave the Hebron massif to seek 'water and grass' on the coastal plain of Shephelah.
2. First theophany: Yahweh confirms to Isaac the promise made to his father Abraham. At Gerar, the doublet of Sarah's adventure occurs, with Rebekah as heroine.
3. Return of the clan to Beersheeba, bringing back into use the old wells dug on this route by Abraham.
4. Second theophany. Yahweh blesses Isaac. Isaac digs a well at Beersheba and there establishes his camp. From Beersheba Jacob, after his difference with his brother Esau, was to leave for Haran in Upper Mesopotamia.

its swarms of animal-headed idols. Consequently, at this point Yahweh intervened. He appeared to Isaac and said, *'Do not go down into Egypt: stay in the land I shall tell you of. Remain for the present here in this land, and I will be with you and bless you. For it is to you and your descendants that I will give all these lands, and I will fulfil the oath I swore to your father Abraham. I will make your descendants as many as the stars of heaven,* [3] *and I will give them all these lands; and all the nations in the world shall bless themselves by your descendants in return for Abraham's obedience; for he kept my charge, my commandments, my statutes and my laws'* (Gen. 26: 2–5). After this warning Isaac remained at Gerar.

When the rainy season came the clan left Shephelah, where they never felt at home, and hurried back to their territory in the Negeb. *From here [Gerar] he went up to Beersheba. Yahweh appeared to him that night and said:*

'I am the God of your father Abraham.
Do not be afraid, for I am with you.
I will bless you and make your descendants many in number on account of my servant Abraham.'

The striking difference between the explosive revelations made to Abraham and the mild words here addressed to Isaac is obvious. Yahweh reassures the young patriarch and reminds him of the promises to Abraham, but he is careful to state clearly that it is on account of his father Abraham that Isaac has been granted so far-reaching a blessing. Quite clearly, Isaac, who is already unobtrusive enough at the human level, does not appear to be called by Yahweh to play a leading role in the adventure of the Chosen People.

It is no less clear, nonetheless, that these events

---

[3] Yahweh had already said to Abraham, *I will make your descendants as many as the stars of heaven and the grains of sand on the seashore* (Gen. 22: 17).

described with telling detail, bear all the marks of authenticity. There is no systematic apology, no attempt at embellishment; on the contrary. Thus despite the fact that he is not outstanding, Isaac appears as a living personality in the pages of the Bible.

The story-teller's difficulty

The story-tellers who before the tents in the cool of the evening were given the responsibility of relating Isaac's life, found the theme somewhat uninspiring. Since there was a lack of interesting anecdotes they solved the difficulty by lifting picturesque events from Abraham's life where they abounded.

In particular, there was one story which, in those primitive times, was very popular; it concerned the trick played by Abraham on two occasions when he camped in a foreign land; it was to ensure his own safety and to obtain the favours of the ruler.

The first occasion was in Egypt or, rather, when the Hebrew clan settled on the eastern approaches to the Nile delta. Fleeing from the famine ravaging the Negeb the Hebrews appeared at the Egyptian frontiers to 'ask for water'. Abraham, realizing that his wife Sarah was beautiful in appearance and that when the Egyptians saw her they would kill him to obtain her for the ruler, instructed her to say that she was his sister [4] so that his life should be saved and he would obtain certain advantages on her account. Events turned out as he had foreseen: on the arrival of the caravan at the edge of the delta Egyptian officials noticed Sarah's beauty and without delay sent her off to Pharaoh's harem. Subsequently the alleged brother was heaped with gifts. But the trick was promptly discovered (probably by the powerful

[4] Sarah, if not the sister, was at least the half-sister of Abraham. They both had the same father (Terah), but not the same mother. Mesopotamian law of this period allowed this kind of marriage. Later Deuteronomy forbade it.

police organization) and Sarah was sent back to her husband.

The story was too good a one not to be used again. Thus we find that much later during a very hot summer Abraham was once more obliged to leave the Negeb. He led his flocks towards the green grass of Gerar where at that time a certain Abimelech was reigning. The Egyptian episode was repeated, but with the difference that on this occasion the warning came from Yahweh who informed Abimelech in a dream that he must return the woman to her husband. Abimelech, who had not touched Sarah, hastened to comply with this supernatural order. Leading biblical commentators are agreed in regarding this passage as a 'doublet' based on the Egyptian episode.

There seemed no reason why this anecdote, which the Semite shepherds found very attractive, since it showed the Egyptians or the Philistines at a disadvantage, should not be incorporated in the life of Isaac, which was lacking in interesting stories. And so we find Isaac and Rebekah in their turn, and for the needs of the cause, as the heroes of this little story. The event is located at Gerar in the same region where Abraham had previously stayed. Still in Isaac's time the country appears to be under the rule of an Abimelech! The same place, the same ruler, an almost identical course of events; once more we are faced with an obvious doublet.

Finally, to give a little more body to the story of Isaac, the story-teller recalled a series of altercations between Isaac's shepherds and those of Abimelech about the ownership of certain wells. These squabbles among Bedouins leave the twentieth-century reader a little cold, but it was by no means the same for the shepherds of those days: the possession of a water supply was absolutely vital. So we can be sure the group of shepherds hung on the lips of the story-teller as he related the course of the arguments. At one place Isaac's men protested heatedly, shouting out 'That water is ours', and the patriarch named the well *Esek* ('quarrel'). On another day there was a further quarrel, again for the possession of a well which the Hebrew shepherds had dug: this one was called *Sitnah* ('accusation'). Lastly, Isaac's shepherds dug another well about which there was no argument this time: it was named *Rehoboth* ('room', 'space').

The story of Isaac is set before us with no great outstanding event and in a rather colourless way; that of his son Jacob was to be far more lively and far more astonishing.

2

JACOB CALLED ISRAEL

The life of Jacob-Israel, the third biblical patriarch, is set before us in a vivid, brisk and colourful narrative. But, in typically eastern fashion, it is rather formless; if this complex adventure of a new and important character in the annals of Israel is to be seen with any clarity, it requires division into three sections:

Jacob in his father's camp

At the outset Jacob is a rather disturbing youth, engrossed in ensuring material possessions for himself, often by underhand methods which even in those days were hardly to be commended.

Jacob: the long round-trip from Bethel to Bethel

Now begins the progressive discovery of the important mission to which one day he was to be called by the Lord. Between two successive revelations are interposed twenty hard years of service in the Upper Euphrates with his uncle Laban, whose two daughters, Leah and Rachel, he married.

Jacob: the new patriarch

After the death of his father Isaac Jacob returned to the Negeb and assumed the leadership of the clan. In accordance with the commands given him by Yahweh he had now to preserve intact the precious spiritual deposit, the idea of the one God.

It is a drama in three acts, each of a distinctly different character. The first is rather anecdotal, the second often moving and the third is imbued with greatness.

Jacob in his father's camp

Here we are in touch with the daily lives of the biblical patriarchs. It is an eventful story interspersed with familiar tales of a somewhat intractable nature. All this is set against the background of the pastoral countryside of southern Palestine.

Isaac and Rebekah await an heir (Gen. 25)

After many years of marriage Isaac and Rebekah still awaited the birth of an heir. To have no children was a great affliction and even a disgrace for an oriental. It was also a continual worry for Isaac, son of Abraham, to whom Yahweh had entrusted an important mission, promising him numerous descendants as the reward for bringing it to a successful conclusion. And now it seemed that Rebekah was barren. Then events took a dramatic turn. Yahweh at last heard Isaac's prayer and Rebekah became pregnant. But things did not seem much better because, as the Bible tells us, *the children struggled with one another inside her, and she said, 'If this is the way of it, why go on living?'* It must have been a very difficult pregnancy. *So she went to consult Yahweh, and he said to her:*

> *'There are two nations in your womb,*
> *Your issue will be two rival peoples.* [1]

[1] The two twins (Esau, the elder; Jacob, the younger) were the founders of two tribes which later separated. Esau, called Edom, was to be leader of the Edomites who settled to the south of the Dead Sea, and on this account this region was called the land of Edom. Jacob, called Israel, was to be the ancestor of the twelve tribes, each formed by the descendants of his twelve sons; the twelve tribes of Israel were to occupy the Promised Land.

One nation shall have the mastery of the other, [2]
and the elder shall serve the younger.'

It seemed that great struggles were to be expected.

Rebekah gives birth to twins

The midwife took care to tie a red cord to the wrist of
the child who appeared first; thus, later, when the question of succeeding his father arose, he could claim the
rights of the first born. We know nowadays that physiologically the elder of twins is the one who is born last. In
antiquity they were less well informed.

On this occasion Rebekah gave birth first to a fine boy
who was red and very hairy, *as though he was completely
wrapped in a hairy cloak*. He was at once called Esau.
Subsequently he became a skilled hunter, *a man of the
open country*. He was not a man of acute mind and was
rather uncouth in his behaviour.

Then Rebekah gave birth to the second twin, Jacob.
He was a beautiful baby with the delicate features
characteristic of his race. In the years to come he was to
appear as an astute and clever diplomat. Unlike his
brother, he felt strongly attracted to life with the flocks
and became the typical peace-loving shepherd, a good
though crafty and astute administrator.

We do not know the meaning of Esau, but as he had
red hair (a colour not appreciated in the East) he was
given the other name of Edom (the 'red-haired'). The
name Jacob is a shortened form of *Ya'aqob-El* which
can be translated 'May God protect!' But the oriental,
always fond of a pun, preferred a more popular explanation. The story was told that Jacob (*Ya'aqob*) was born

---

[2] In the time of King David (800 years after this prophecy) the Edomites were
conquered and annexed by the Israelites. It may well be wondered whether the
'prophecy' did not take shape at that time.

21

This could be Esau.

with his hand grasping his twin's heel (*'aqeb*). So we are not to be surprised if one day Jacob (*Ya'aqob*) supplants (*ya'aqab*) his brother Esau. Etymologies of this kind appealed to the Hebrew shepherds.

Thus we are shown the appearance on the scene of two brothers hostile to each other, of two protagonists very dissimilar in their physical features as in their different vocations. To complicate the situation even further Esau seemed to be the favourite of his father Isaac, to whom he regularly brought the produce of his hunting. Jacob, on the other hand, was the favourite of his mother whose side he scarcely left.

The trick to obtain the inheritance

The Hebrew shepherds never grew tired of listening to tales of the tricks that Jacob, the artful shepherd, played on the loutish Esau, the hunter. One day Jacob had just made for himself a sort of lentil soup which smelt very appetizing. Esau came on the scene, just back from a hunting expedition, hungry and exhausted. He went into his brother's tent and said: *'Let me eat the red soup, that red soup there; I am exhausted' — hence the name given to him, Edom.* [3]

Jacob, who was shrewd and cunning, had an easy task in dealing with the uncouth Esau. He willingly agreed to give his brother the soup which he had just made, but on condition that Esau made over to Jacob his birthright (as the elder). Without hesitation Esau promised on oath what his younger brother had asked. *And after eating and drinking he got up and went. That was all*

[3] Another pun. As we know already, Esau was red-haired. In addition we find him now eating the red soup. From this he was given the nickname of *Edom* (the red). All this betrays a biassed view with all the elements of caricature. At the time when these passages were written (five or six centuries before Christ) the Edomites were the avowed enemies of the Israelites.

Esau cared for his birthright. [4] is the comment in Genesis (a Yahwistic passage this one) which endeavours to show the right on Jacob's side since he was the ancestor of the twelve tribes of Israel. In this first public appearance Jacob gives us the impression of being certainly very intelligent but rather wily.

Esau's unfortunate marriages

We know how important the Aramean shepherds considered the question of racial purity. The nomads of these tribes took care to choose their wives from a clan related to them. And we saw all the precautions taken by Abraham when the question arose of marrying his son Isaac; from Hebron, the pastoral centre in the south of Palestine, he sent Eliezer, his trusted servant, to Haran in the great northern elbow of the Euphrates. Haran was in fact the assembly point for the Aramean tribes scattered over the pasturelands of Mesopotamia and the Mediterranean countries which one day were to form Palestine, Lebanon, Syria and Jordania.

When the biblical patriarchs became the guardians of the Revelation still less could there be any question of making an ill-chosen match with the Canaanites or Egyptian women, or even with women belonging to primitive non-Semitic peoples. Esau, indeed, seems to have had no understanding of the problem at all; he began in fact by marrying two Hittites. [5] We may well imagine the pain caused to Isaac and Rebekah by the

---

[4] The laws of primogeniture, or the birthright, among the Sumerians as among the Akkadians, whose legislation was followed by the biblical patriarchs, were of Mesopotamian origin, and have nothing in common with western practice in this connection. It was much less exclusive. In the East, when the paternal inheritance was shared out the law laid down that the eldest should receive a share that was double that given to the younger brothers. In certain cases it was allowed that on his own authority (and it was considerable) the father of the family could transfer this right, called the birthright, to a younger son of his choice.

[5] At this period (about 1800 B.C.) there were no Hittites in the land of Canaan. Hurrite women, a non-Semitic people, must be meant here.

matrimonial policy adopted by their elder son, hitherto regarded as the future chieftain of the Hebrew clan, who was to be responsible for the lofty spiritual mission entrusted by Yahweh to Abraham and his descendants.

The theft of the paternal blessing

With a plate of lentil soup, Jacob by a trick had easily succeeded in acquiring the birthright. But this transaction gave him no grounds for thinking that at the death of his father Isaac the paternal inheritance would automatically fall to him. In fact, a new chief of the clan could not take up the staff of government without previously receiving his father's blessing, for only the blessing of his father had the power of inducting the man of his choice to his new religious and secular functions.

In the ancient east the blessing given by the patriarch to his successor was bestowed with imposing poetic formulas. God by pouring out his benefits on men had blessed them. By the same token, the chieftains who represented God possessed in their turn the power of blessing those who were subject to their authority. And the best way of wishing someone well was, on a final analysis, by giving expression to the desire that he should be blessed by God.

Now Jacob, in the circumstances, appeared to have no chance at all of receiving this blessing. But that was no obstacle to Jacob and his mother. To obtain their ends they formed a plan of a truly Machiavellian kind.

One day Isaac, who now scarcely left his bed, asked for his son Esau. Rebekah, who kept careful watch over the interests of her younger son, understood that an important moment had arrived. And so, through the slits secretly contrived in the cloth forming the partitions in the tent, she made ready to follow very closely the conversation between the two men.

Esau arrived. Isaac, feeling his age, complained that he was on the threshold of the grave,[6] but that before dying he would like to enjoy a dish of game. He requested his hunter son to take his quiver and his bow and to go into the neighbouring country and hunt a deer. Then Esau was to make it ready for his father. In conclusion, Isaac promised to bestow his blessing upon him, endowing him with the political and religious leadership of the clan.

Rebekah hastened to warn her favourite son Jacob and told him what to do: *'Go to the flock, and bring me back two good kids, so that I can make the kind of savoury your father likes. Then you can take it to your father for him to eat so that he may bless you before he dies.'*

Jacob put forward certain timid objections. He explained *'My brother Esau is hairy, while I am smooth-skinned. If my father happens to touch me, he will see I am cheating him, and I shall bring down a curse on myself instead of a blessing.'* Rebekah quickly replied that Jacob should concern himself with the two animals to be killed and that she would see to cooking them. If by some mischance the trick did not succeed Rebekah would take on herself the curse which might be threatening her son.

When the dish had been carefully prepared (a matter of importance seeing Isaac's particular preference) Rebekah went to Esau's tent. There she took his best clothes and quickly dressed Jacob in them, taking care at the same time to pull over the young man's neck and

---

[6] In fact we find his death recorded a good twenty years after this scene, when Jacob came back from Paddan Naharaiim (in the region of Haran) where he had served his uncle Laban, his mother Rebekah's brother. It is probable that these two accounts (one belongs to the Elohistic cycle, the other to the Yahwistic) have here been conflated without the scribe responsible for the definitive version taking care to rectify certain contradictory elements.

arms the tufts of goat hair with which this rough and primitive cloak was covered. Then she placed the tastily cooked dish in Jacob's hands and urged him towards his father's tent.

Jacob began by bowing low before Isaac and announced his presence by saying *'Father I am here.'*

The oriental who is about to receive a blessing greets the one who has summoned him with great respect. The Hebrew word *berek* (meaning, 'bend the knee'; it is also used for camels which are made to kneel down) shows us clearly the exact attitude adopted in the presence of the representative of God. From certain biblical texts we know that a blessing was given according to a clearly determined ritual: the officiant raised his arms to call down the divine power from on high; he then laid his hands on the head of him on whom divine protection was invoked.

'My father,' Jacob had said. *'Who are you, my son?'* asked the blind man. *'I am Esau, your firstborn,'* boldly declared Jacob, *'I have done as you told me. Please get up and take your place and eat the game I have brought and then give me your blessing.'* The aged patriarch was surprised that the game had been so quickly tracked down and killed. Jacob explained that Yahweh had put it in his path. But Isaac, shrewder than Rebekah had imagined, still appeared distrustful, and wished to feel his son's clothes. *'The voice is Jacob's voice,'* he said, *'but the arms are the arms of Esau.'* Still he hesitated: *'Are you really my son, Esau?'* he inquired. *'I am,'* replied the impostor. *'Bring it here,'* said Isaac, *'that I may eat the game my son has brought, and so may give you my blessing.'* And when he had eaten it, he commanded, *'Come closer, and kiss me, my son.'* Isaac, who still seemed worried, smelt his clothes. And then, without

27

more ado he began to give his blessing:

'Yes, the smell of my son
is like the smell of a fertile field blessed by Yahweh.
May God give you
dew from heaven,
and the richness of the earth,
abundance of grain and wine!
May nations serve you
and peoples bow down before you!
Be master of your brothers;
may the sons of your mother bow down before you!
Cursed be he who curses you;
blessed be he who blesses you!'

It may seem surprising that in the first two verses both vocabulary and images owe nothing to a society of wandering shepherds. It is a style derived from an agricultural community: there is mention of a 'fertile field' of 'dew' (and the importance of the morning dew for the cultivators in Palestine during a dry season will be realized), of grain and wine. All this might be explained by the fact that, in addition to the appeal to the goodness of God, the blessings of the patriarchs consisted of prophetic declarations about the future of their descendants. It could be held that here Isaac described, in his foresight of the distant future, scenes from the agricultural existence which after the return from Egypt and penetration into the land of Canaan was to be adopted by the people of Israel. But this may well be a place where a later scribe has expanded Isaac's blessing to fit the conditions of the scribe's own times.

And now the trick had been played. After seizing the birthright from Esau, Jacob had now obtained by fraud the solemn blessing from Isaac which was the prerogative of the legal heir.

Esau's reaction (Gen. 27: 30–40)

Just as Jacob was going out Esau returned and went into his father, and with some ceremony set before him a dish of venison, saying: *'Father, get up and eat the game your son has brought and then give me your blessing.'* The old man was painfully surprised, and when he saw that he had been tricked by Jacob he was seized with a great trembling. To the best of his ability he explained how his good faith had been abused: *'Your brother came by fraud and took your blessing.'*

According to the religious law of Mesopotamia a blessing (or indeed a curse) was irrevocable. At the time of the patriarchs a blessing was regarded as a magic formula containing its own efficacy. Once it had been given a blessing remained what it was; it was impossible to change its conditions, modify its clauses or revoke them. *'Father, bless me, too!'* exclaimed Esau loudly and bitterly. Isaac remained silent. Esau insisted: *'First he took my birthright, and look, now he has taken my blessing! Have you not kept a blessing for me?'* Isaac shook his head. *'See,'* he said, *'I have made him your master; I have given him all his brothers as servants, . . . What can I do for you, my son?'* In fact, he could do nothing, for the ideas prevailing among the nomads at that time did not allow a blessing to be annulled, even if given in error. But Esau insisted the more strongly: *'Was that your only blessing, father? Father, give me a blessing too.'* Isaac remained silent. Then Esau burst into tears.

Then suddenly Isaac began to speak. He prophesied, describing what was to be the harsh life of his dispossessed heir, a consequence of the new legal and religious situation:

*'Far from the riches of the earth
shall be your dwelling place,*

far from the dew that falls from heaven.[7]
You shall live by your sword[8]
and you shall serve your brother.[9]
But when you win your freedom, you shall take his yoke from your neck.[10]

For Esau it meant the collapse of his dreams. He was a man of primitive instincts and quickly found the answer to his brother's treachery. It seemed probable that the patriarch's death was near at hand; directly it had occurred Esau determined to kill his brother. And he made no mystery of his intention to anyone. Among primitive tribes vengeance was one of the forms of justice.

Flight, the only solution for Jacob

Obviously it was not long before Rebekah heard of her son Esau's bloodthirsty plan. And so she could expect to lose two sons in succession: Jacob from Esau's promised vengeance; Esau condemned by the blood-law. As a far-seeing woman she promptly found a solution, at least a temporary one. Jacob was to set out as soon as possible for Haran and take refuge with his uncle, her brother Laban. As time went on Esau's anger would cool. She could then have her favourite son brought back to take up the chieftainship of the clan.

It was difficult to explain the true situation to the blind

[7] This detail refers to the endemic drought in the land of Edom (formerly Seir, open land unsuitable for agriculture). This country is situated to the south of the Dead Sea, to the east of the wadi el-Araba.

[8] *By your sword:* that is by hunting, by plundering and brigandage, in contrast to the peaceful and honourable civilization of the pastoral groups with their flocks of sheep and their goats.

[9] Isaac foretells in this prophetic utterance that during its history Edom is to be more or less subject to the domination of the sons of Jacob.

[10] The last phrase is in prose. Some commentators believe that it was added to the biblical text at a much later period – under Joram, king of Judah (872–842), husband of the famous Athaliah, when Edom successfully revolted against Judaean control.

man, but with a further good lie she would manage to get over the difficulty. She went to her husband, and reminded him of the unfortunate marriages contracted by Esau. At all costs, she said, Jacob must be prevented from following his brother's example. In these circumstances she suggested that Jacob should be sent to Paddan Naharaiim, to the 'Land of the Fathers', that region of the Upper Euphrates where the Aramean stock remained pure. There Jacob would be able to choose a wife from among the daughters of his uncle Laban and in this way the blood of the future patriarch would be preserved from any impurity. No sooner said than done. Jacob received a further blessing, confirming the first. He put on his sandals and girded his loins with the traditional cloth, took his staff (his only possession) and with a heavy heart, as we may well believe, set out for the north and the land of exile.

Moral judgement on young Jacob

As a general rule the modern reader of the Bible experiences a certain scandalized surprise at the strange behaviour of Jacob at the time when he was still living under his father's tents. The biblical historian can here offer a little explanation.

It must be recognized quite frankly in the first place that at the period in question the level of moral conscience was by no means high. In fact we ought to be grateful to the successive writers, who one after another recorded this pastoral tradition, that they did not give way to the temptation to improve the impression produced by the character they were describing. With the best of intentions an author might obviously have endeavoured to show us Jacob far more advantageously, and especially, more in accordance with the social and religious laws of a more evolved period. Fortunately no efforts have been

31

made in this sense. The story is primitive, untouched, we can see it in all its crudity. And that is an excellent proof of its authenticity.

Indeed a watered-down version of the facts would have had serious consequences. It is the purpose of the Bible to relate for us the adventure of the Chosen People, going forward under the guidance of Yahweh. On a final analysis, the history of Israel is the spiritual development of a human group endeavouring to raise itself to a higher stage. This spiritual ideal untiringly pursued by Israel is a thing unheard of in any religion of antiquity. No priestly college, whether Mesopotamian or Egyptian, was concerned to send forth its adepts onto the steep path of moral perfection, ceaselessly in course of evolution. The People of God was the only one to set out on this route; for them it was long and painful, punctuated by distressing falls and heroic recoveries. And we should remember here that, in the Christian view, this uneven progress which began with Abraham, was to find its logical fulfilment in the law of Christ.

Jacob took the path leading to Haran. He had certainly not yet learned to control his earthly appetites which for some time were to continue to smother the voice of his conscience. But soon Yahweh was to speak to him. And, when he had understood the message, Jacob the shepherd was to become Israel the patriarch.

From Bethel to Bethel

The first part of Jacob's life, which we have just been looking at, appears to have no religious side to it at all. He seems to be almost entirely concerned with his material interests and indeed scarcely troubled by spiritual problems. With the second chapter of his life, which we are now beginning, there is a change of outlook: quite unexpectedly Yahweh seems to invade this soul which hitherto had appeared closed to higher things.

The first appearance of Yahweh to Jacob occurred on the steppes of Bethel when alone and a fugitive. His sole possession his shepherd's staff, Jacob was on his way to Haran. There, with no preparation, Yahweh revealed to the traveller that one day he would be entrusted with the Promise, the famous Promise already given and confirmed on various occasions to his grandfather Abraham and his father Isaac.

The second appearance of Yahweh to Jacob took place at Bethel again, but twenty years later. At that time Jacob was on the return journey from his long sojourn with his uncle Laban in Haran in the region of the Two Rivers. There he had married: his two wives and two concubines had given him eleven sons (he was shortly to have a twelfth); he possessed a number of slaves, large flocks of sheep and goats and even some camels. It was no longer the poor shepherd whom we observed previously in this same place. On this second time of passing through Bethel Yahweh appeared again to remind Jacob of his plans for him and for his descendants.

Between the first halt at Bethel and the camp there on the return journey there was an interval of twenty years. During this there occurred his time as a shepherd at Haran, a somewhat turbulent and dramatic period, passed at his uncle Laban's, Rebekah's brother. This is a period of historical importance for the Hebrew people, their genealogy and the constitution of the social framework of the People of God. And it is of considerable importance also because here we observe the spiritual transformation of Jacob the father of twelve eponymous heroes, the future leaders of the twelve tribes of Israel.

During this period we follow Jacob's strange adventures; they can be divided as follows:

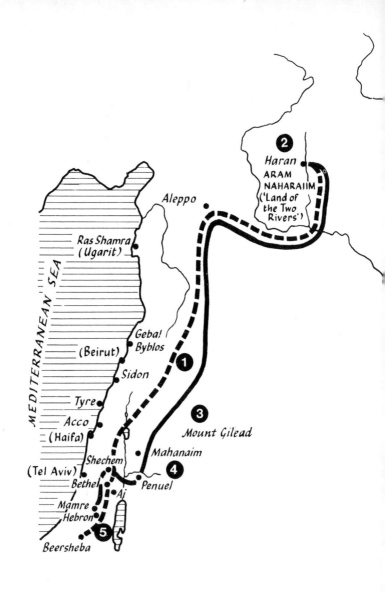

JACOB'S JOURNEY: BEERSHEBA – HARAN – MAMRE

1. The dotted line shows Jacob's outward journey from Beersheba to Haran, in the Land of the Fathers, in the Upper Euphrates. The only halt mentioned by the Bible in this journey of about 700 miles was at Bethel (Jacob's dream, the revelations of Yahweh).

2. At Haran (Paddan-aram = the land of Aram or Aram Naharaiim = Aram of the Two Rivers; the Hebrews also called it the Land of the Fathers), Jacob served his uncle Laban whose two daughters he married. He remained there seven years, then a further seven and then six. Then with his wives and his flocks he set out on the return journey to Hebron.

3. At Mount Gilead (the future Mount Ephraim) Laban caught up with his nephew Jacob (who was also his brother-in-law) to ask the reason for his sudden departure. A treaty was drawn up between Laban and Jacob.

4. The ford over the Jabbok. Before crossing the stream Jacob had a vision at Mahanaim (the two camps), renamed Peniel, or 'the face of God'. Next a halt at Succoth and crossing of the Jordan. Then he settled at Shechem. After the Dinah-Shechem affair, hasty departure for Bethel. Settlement at Bethel.

5. From Bethel at the oaks of Mamre near Hebron the caravan rejoined the camp of the old patriarch Isaac who, as he died, made Jacob his heir.

Jacob on the way to Haran; the dream at Bethel.
Jacob in the service of his uncle Laban.
Jacob leaves the Land of the Fathers.
Jacob's spiritual transformation at the ford of the Jabbok and at Bethel.
Jacob returns to his father's tents.

The dream at Bethel

Daily Jacob drew farther away from his father's camp at Beersheba. Suddenly, at one of the first stages Yahweh came to him. It seems that to reveal himself to Jacob and to make his mission clear to him, Yahweh waited for him to be at a distance from the family circle where questions of self-interest predominated, where there were continual clashes and material concerns took pride of place. We see now the plan which Yahweh puts before the man whom he has decided to entrust with the Promise. And we see, too, the reaction of this Hebrew shepherd who, it must be admitted, seems unfitted to become one day the 'man of God'.

Jacob's dream

The sun had set. Taking one of the stones to be found at that place, he made it his pillow and lay down where he was.

This was an old custom of the Semitic shepherds accustomed to spend the night in the open. He used a stone for a pillow, but covered it, of course, with the end of his ample woollen cloak. *He had a dream: a ladder was there, standing on the ground with its top reaching to heaven; and there were angels of God going up it and coming down. And Yahweh was there, standing over him, and saying, 'I am Yahweh, the God of Abraham your father, and the God of Isaac'* (Gen. 28: 12–13).

Before going further there is need for explanation. Architecturally, in the first place: what exactly was this 'ladder', at first sight a rather unusual term? From the historical point of view this processional going up and down between 'heaven' and 'earth', belongs, as we shall see, to an old Sumerian rite. But from the spiritual point of view, the whole picture takes on an entirely new symbolic meaning.

Thus there are three points needing examination.

Jacob's ladder

At the beginning of the previous volume *Abraham, Loved by God,* a chapter was devoted to the time he spent in the region of Ur in Lower Mesopotamia. Something was said there of the Sumerian ziggurats, the enormous buildings, like pyramids with steps, whose solid silhouette rose out of the centre of each city-state.

The ziggurat, we may recall, was a rectangular building in brick, with three storeys, standing back from each other, reached by huge external staircases. The height of these great superimposed blocks might be as much as 195 feet. Right at the top, on the last platform there was a *cella* in which was to be found the statue of the tutelary deity of the city. This chapel was known in the Sumerian ritual as 'heaven'.

Abraham, who used to graze his flocks on the thin grassy belt between the cultivated land and the wilderness, was familiar with the ziggurat of Ur, dominating the whole conglomeration of houses, palaces and temples. In addition, during the long journey undertaken by Abraham with his clan, going up the valley of the Euphrates, from Ur to Haran, the Hebrew shepherds would have been able to see a number of these high towers in the distance.

These buildings had been put up at the cost of thousands upon thousands of human lives, of labourers forced to carry the bricks and work under threat of the whip.

As a result the Mesopotamian ziggurats were held in horror by the Hebrews, for they, too, could be press-ganged on occasion to work on these hated buildings. In any case, and especially since the time when at Haran Yahweh revealed to Abraham and his clan the idea of the one God, the ziggurat appeared to them as the very symbol of idolatry.

In the previous volume it was explained how the ziggurat of Babylon (*Bab-ili,* 'gate of the gods') could have given rise in the shepherds' camps to the fable known as the tower of Babel. These shepherds regarded these enormous buildings as an expression of the pride of men who, in a fit of madness, decided to climb up to heaven and drive out God. But 'heaven' as we have seen was the Sumerian name for the *cella* at the top of the building. This detail enables us to see how the nomads had misunderstood the matter.

To obtain access to the successive platforms the ritual processions organized by the Sumerian priests made their way up the imposing stairways. In addition, at certain periods of the year, the priests solemnly brought down the statue of the god of the city. And this may explain for us, perhaps, the architectural setting of Jacob's vision: *a ladder . . . standing on the ground with its top reaching to heaven.* For a primitive nomad shepherd a stairway was probably a constructional element difficult to imagine. In the present case, it was obviously expressed by the word 'ladder', a primitive tool that everyone knew.

The sumptuous procession carrying the deity down the immense exterior stairways of the ziggurat, the slow and solemn return of the priests up to the *cella* called heaven — the ascent and descent of the angels seen by Jacob in his dream: these are two images which bear a close relationship. And thus we have a probable explanation of Jacob's vision by means of its archaeological context.

What is the symbolic explanation of the *angels of God* (that is, the Spirit of God) going up and coming down – a continuous, untiring movement in both directions on the imposing stairway bringing heaven and earth into communication?

Here the traditional exegesis of the passage proves acceptable. There is revealed to us by this vivid picture a theological idea that was original at this period, namely, the continual, providential manifestation of God in the lives of men. Hitherto, in the ancient religions there was only the blind, implacable action of the various deities of the pantheon, exercising their power fatalistically over the earth. Now with the story of Jacob's ladder can be seen the beginning of a mystical relationship between the believer and his Creator. Henceforth, there is established a stream of spiritual graces between God and his faithful creatures. Man can now communicate with God in his heart. And he can do so otherwise than by the rites of pagan sacrifice, based on the material idea of 'a gift for a gift': for the offering of an ox some earthly advantage was given in exchange.

The 'ladder', the twofold column of angels moving unceasingly between God and his creatures, is the sign of a profound spiritual advance.

'God needs men'

Jacob's dream does not end at this point.

And Yahweh was there, standing over him, and saying, 'I am Yahweh, the God of Abraham your father, and the God of Isaac. I will give to you and your descendants the land on which you are lying. Your descendants shall be like the specks of dust on the ground; you shall spread to the west and the east, to the north and the south, and all the tribes of the earth shall bless themselves by you and your descendants' (Gen. 28: 13–14).

And so the Covenant was renewed. There is nothing surprising or original in this confirmation of the Promise already clearly stated in solemn form, first to Abraham and then to Isaac. Jacob was merely informed that it was through his descendants that the Promise was to be effected; it was for him now to do his part.

Yahweh certainly did not confine himself to this reminder. He summoned Jacob in person, declared his trust in him, and promised him help and protection. *'Be sure that I am with you; I will keep you safe wherever you go, and bring you back to this land, for I will not desert you before I have done all that I have promised you.'* At first sight, probably, and looking at the matter from the purely human viewpoint, Yahweh's choice may seem surprising; Jacob, with his cunning tricks, sly conduct and shameless lying, hardly seems to us to be of the stuff of a hero worthy of Yahweh's attention and fitted to be designated as Abraham's and Isaac's successor.

In the Old Testament, like the New, we are often surprised by some unexpected choice on God's part. Thus at the beginning of the story of Paul of Tarsus, the savage persecutor of the first Christians, who could have expected to see him suddenly become the apostle destined to carry the message of Jesus across the Near East and as far as Italy? God calls to himself those he will send by gauging their temperament, their intelligence, shrewdness and effective possibilities. Esau the elder (or at least the supposed elder) was in reality unfit and rather limited. Now by doing violence to moral principles Jacob gave evidence of his possibilities as a man of action. It was he who was chosen. For the time being Yahweh left him a free hand. But when the time came, twenty years later at the ford of Jabbok, shortly before his second halt at Bethel, Yahweh was responsible for the spiritual transformation of the man whom he had chosen.

Jacob's awakening

Then Jacob awoke from his sleep and said, 'Truly, Yahweh is in this place and I never knew it!' He was afraid and said, 'How awe-inspiring this place is! This is nothing less than a house of God; this is the gate of heaven!' (Gen. 28: 16–17). Jacob's reaction was one of terror, in the pagan sense: fear experienced in the presence of a divine manifestation whose reality is undeniable (*'Yahweh is in this place'*); fear at the unexpected nature of the apparition (*'and I never knew it!'*); lastly, fear of this place, this piece of earth, henceforward to be held sacred, on which Yahweh, the God of his ancestors, had just manifested himself. All this is in harmony with the pagan religions of antiquity. Jacob's spiritual evolution was not yet sufficiently advanced to enable him to answer God's call as Abraham, his grandfather, had done by an act of faith and immediate, complete and generous acceptance.

Jacob puts up a stele which he names beth-El, or 'house of God' (Gen. 28: 18–19)

This is a further feature derived from the Canaanite religion, but from a remoter age, since it was a question of the erection of a 'standing stone', what is called in the West a menhir. This ritual act carried out by Jacob cannot be understood without some preliminary explanation.

During the prehistoric period mysterious Indo-European tribes swarmed into the West. Archaeology is in a position to follow their migrations owing to the fact that wherever they settled they erected megaliths in accordance with rules that were laid down fairly strictly. We have knowledge of the various ways in which these stones were put up. There was the isolated stone (menhir), and also the simple heap of boulders (cairn), built to fix a boundary between two spheres of influence and to ratify a sort of peace treaty. More complicated were the stones placed in lines (e.g. Karnak, Morbihan). Sometimes, also, they were arranged in a circle (Stonehenge, in England). Lastly, when one or more slabs were laid upon high vertical stones this primitive architectural form is known as a dolmen.

In ancient Asia and particularly in what is now Palestine and Jordania these types of megalithic construction were to be found. Were the invaders who, between 4500 and 4000 B.C. (approximate dates), settled in the Mediterranean Near East Indo-Europeans? Or did they belong to a Hittite branch? In the present state of our knowledge this is a question of some difficulty. In any case, we have here the cult of the standing stone introduced among the civilizations of the Near East.

Already, well before Abraham's arrival in Palestine, the Canaanites (a Semitic race and, we should remember, closely related to the Hebrews) who were the previous occupiers of the territory, worshipped stones put up in their sacred places, often on the top of mountains under the open sky. Sometimes the stele stood alone; at others several stones were arranged in a line or in a circle (cromlech). This last formation was called by the Hebrews *gilgal* and it gave its name to several sacred places in Palestine *(hag-Gilgal)*.

The Canaanites called the raised stone *beth-El* ('house of God') so we may conclude that these steles were regarded as the dwelling of a supernatural being belonging to the polytheist pantheon. At first the stone stood in the centre of a sanctuary where it constituted the principal object of worship. Subsequently, the raised stone, set up in an open place, was to become a votive stele, a reminder to the deity of a petition made or granted; it could thus become a place of pilgrimage. Gradually in the Semitic world this religion of the raised stone became widespread. In the following centuries we find the Israelites paying homage to the menhirs which Yahweh's faithful subjects venerated as the dwelling-place of their one and invisible God. On this sacred stone it was customary to pour oil, perhaps wine also; incense was burned before it; on it were offered the first fruits of the harvest, the first from a batch of cakes that had been baked; on it were sacrificed the firstborn of the flock.

To summarize: probably this stone cult was of Indo-European origin and brought into the Near East by the migrations. It was then adopted by some of the Semitic tribes, the Canaanites especially, who occupied the territory before the arrival of the Hebrews. On a final analysis it was a pagan cult from which the sons of Abraham, in about 1800 B.C., had not yet been able to rid themselves. Twelve hundred years later, at the time of Jeremiah, and to the prophet's great annoyance, some Israelites still bowed down before these stones saying, *'You have begotten me'* (Jer. 2: 27).

It is not surprising, therefore, to find Jacob when he awoke 'setting up a stele' at the place where Yahweh, the God of Abraham, had spoken to him. To the Almighty, who had just manifested himself, it was fitting to offer a 'dwelling': it would be possible thus on occasion to communicate with him afresh, and if needs be renew the conversation. In accordance with the centuries-old ritual (but this is the first mention of it to be found in the Bible) Jacob poured a little oil over the stone. All this was strictly Canaanite practice.

Jacob's vow

Jacob made this vow, 'If God goes with me and keeps me safe on this journey I am making, if he gives me bread to eat and clothes to wear, and if I return home safely to my father, then Yahweh shall be my God. This stone I have set up as a monument shall be a house of God [beth-El], and I will surely pay you a tenth part of all you give me' (Gen. 28: 20–22).

It is quite clear that the grandson was far from responding to God's advances with the impulsive faith of his grandfather. Indeed, Jacob was still refusing to commit himself to a course of action which appeared to him to be far from clear and perhaps even dangerous. His mind was strongly imbued with paganism: Yahweh must first give proof of his almighty powers and especially of his care for Jacob; he is to furnish food and clothing and bring him back one day safe and sound to Isaac's tents; if Yahweh does all this then he will be Jacob's God. Jacob was still at the stage of 'human wisdom' and perhaps, still more, was inspired by pagan religious ideas to which an act of gratuitous love was entirely incomprehensible and conversation with the deity was strictly confined to bargaining.

The location of Bethel

What was the exact position of Bethel on the map? Already in the life of Abraham we have found the name of Bethel occurring in the Bible at the time when the patriarch, arriving with his flocks from the Aramean centre at Haran, was making his first contact with the Promised Land. At that time, leaving the valley of Shechem, he set out towards Mount Ephraim. *He pitched his tent, with Bethel to the west and Ai to the east. There he built an altar to Yahweh and invoked the name of Yahweh* (Gen. 12: 8). Of course, it is by anticipation that Genesis here speaks of Bethel. Abraham's camp — he returned a little later to the same place — was located, it seems, in a part of the open country without any precise name. In addition, we know that the name of *beth-El* (house of God) was given to this place nearly a hundred years after Abraham by his grandson Jacob.

Both men had halted near the small hamlet of Luz (or Luza) which was surrounded by plantations of almond trees (*Luz*, in Hebrew). The village of Bethel, built at a later date, is today part of the ancient Luz; these two tiny agglomerations form Beitin where the Pittsburg Theological Seminary is carrying out excavations. But was it really at Beitin that Abraham built his altar to Yahweh? Was it there that Jacob raised his stone? Following conclusions of several authors I believe that Bethel was situated on a hill very nearly half a mile from Beitin now known as Khirbet el-Bordj. There may be seen an ancient enclosure some three-quarters of which are in ruins. In the centre is a square courtyard in a state of partial preservation. And, as was mentioned in the previous volume, from this magnificent natural position, at a height of 2,700 feet there is an imposing panorama over the valley of the Jordan, against the background of the darkening wall of the mountains of Moab and Gilead, while to the south can be seen the shining white hills of Judah.

Jacob continues his journey

Bethel is the only halting place mentioned by the Bible during Jacob's long journey to Haran. The fact is of some importance for it chronicles the first of Yahweh's overtures to Jacob, the man of his choice. But Jacob, it must be admitted, does not appear to have understood much of the divine message. It did not matter. With time, and

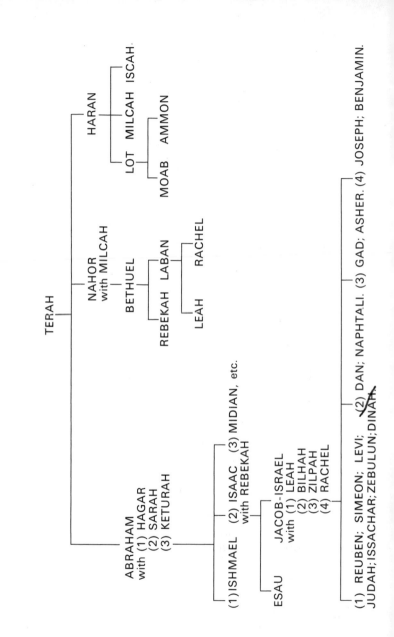

especially after certain sore trials, he managed to grasp the meaning of his mission. Once again we may observe the continually developing character of biblical history.

Jacob at his uncle Laban's home

For the next twenty years Jacob was to serve as a shepherd to his uncle Laban, the chieftain of the Aramean tribe. At the end of his journey into exile the fugitive was warmly welcomed by his relations in the Haran region; he was to marry two of his first cousins and, by the exercise of considerable cunning, managed to amass a large fortune in flocks and slaves.

The territory of Haran, the Aramean centre

When Terah in his old age, accompanied by his son Abraham, had left the land of Ur, in Lower Mesopotamia, to journey with his whole clan to the land of Canaan near the other extremity of the Fertile Crescent, the migration took place in two phases: first, for a fairly long period, the caravan stopped at Haran in the region of the Upper Euphrates; subsequently, after Terah's death, under Abraham's orders, the little band of shepherds set out for the Negeb.

What was the reason for halting in this region which forms a sort of elbow between Mesopotamia and the land of Canaan? In the Bible, this territory, whose principal city is Haran, is called Paddan-aram (the plain of Aram), or Aram Naharaiim (Aram of the Two Rivers, that is the Tigris and the Euphrates). Sometimes the patriarchs called it the Land of the Fathers and, on occasion, the Land of the Sons of the East.

These clans of Aramean nomads were scattered almost everywhere over the immense area of steppe land which extends in a semi-circle from the Persian Gulf to the eastern confines of the Nile delta. Small isolated settlements, jealous of their independance, carefully avoided any possibility of misalliance with other nomads who were 'not of their blood'. There were camps of shepherds continually on the move from one pasture to another, always in search of fresh grass and water. But these wandering shepherds seemed to possess a sort of territorial centre, probably of a religious nature. This was Aram Naharaiim, the Land of the Fathers. Here the Aramean language was to remain for long in use.

We know that Abraham left Haran on the orders of Yahweh who had decided to isolate this tiny Hebrew group, to whom the notion of the one God had just been revealed, far from the other Aramean groups who practised idolatry. Shortly after Abraham's departure, Nahor, Abraham's own brother, arrived in this great elbow of the Euphrates. He too had left the region of Ur to settle in the Land of the Fathers.

Of course, this branch of Terah's family, unaffected by the Revelation, continued to venerate its Babylonian gods. But it did not prevent Abraham's clan, settled in the Negeb, nearly 500 miles away, from remaining in fairly close touch with the Aramean centre (Gen. 22: 20–4). And there is proof of these family ties: when Abraham was looking for a wife for his son Isaac he sent his confidential slave to Paddan-aram to find one among his cousins; and it was Rebekah, the sister of the patriarch Laban, who was providentially chosen. So now it was the turn of Jacob, Rebekah's son, to return to the Land of the Fathers to take a wife, thus enabling him, as the future Hebrew chieftain who had been blessed by his father at Hebron and entrusted with his mission by Yahweh at Bethel, to preserve the purity of the race, a sacred principle among the Arameans.

Importance of the well as a meeting place

At this period in the Near East there were two normal places for meeting. One of them was the city gate: here were the court of law and the traders' stalls, here there gathered the gossips and those with nothing to do. Thus, when Abraham wanted to buy the cave Machpelah to make it into a family burial place, he went to the gate of Hebron and there, as if by chance, encountered the owner of the site. But among the shepherds there was a still more favoured spot for meetings. This was the well where, after the heat of the day, the shepherds led their flocks to water them.

These wells were often quite wide, anything from ten to fifteen feet in diameter. To prevent pollution of the water the opening was closed during the day with one or more flat stone slabs. A low surrounding wall prevented the animals from falling in the well. When the time came the shepherds drew the water in skins which they pulled up with cords. It was then poured into stone or earthenware troughs. In turn the flocks, each under its own shepherd, came to quench their thirst. At the end of the day, then, each well became a meeting place where news was exchanged and a stranger could obtain information.

The meeting between Jacob and Rachel

Jacob was now getting to the end of his long journey. After fording the Euphrates he continued along the bank of the Balikh, a tributary of the Euphrates and then of the Kara, a tributary of the Balikh. And so he came to Paddan-aram. As an experienced traveller in this kind of country he sought a track leading to a well. On the ground, well trodden by sheep and goats, a practised eye easily discovered the path to be followed. Soon he came upon a group of shepherds watching over their flocks and gathered round a well. According to custom they waited until all the flocks had assembled; only then was the great boulder closing the well rolled away and the animals watered. After the customary ceremonial greetings Jacob talked to the shepherds. They told him that they came from Haran, that they were well acquainted with Laban and that he was still head of the clan of Terah. *'And here,'* added one of the shepherds, *'comes his daughter Rachel with the sheep.'*

Rachel was extremely beautiful; at first sight of her Jacob lost his heart. As she drew near he hastened to roll away the heavy stone from the mouth of the well then, with no word of explanation he set about drawing water and filling the troughs for his uncle's flock to drink. With some surprise, and perhaps with a certain secret emotion, the girl considered this attentive stranger. After the sheep had quenched their thirst Jacob went up to Rachel. He kissed her, Genesis tells us, and burst into tears. Then he told her that he was Laban's nephew and therefore her cousin. At once Rachel hastened to Haran to tell her father.

Directly Laban heard of the unexpected arrival of his sister's son he hurried to the well where his nephew was waiting. He kissed him warmly and with the traditional signs of friendship asked him to come to his house.

Mention of Laban's house shows us that he did not live in a tent as, traditionally, the shepherds did. In this region of rich pastureland watered by numerous streams it was usual for a chieftain, the wealthy owner of flocks, to live in a house in a city, while his shepherds in charge of his flocks went from pasture to pasture with their flocks, and lived, of course, in tents. Indeed, even nowadays it is interesting to observe that the Bedouin chiefs, as a general rule, choose to live in houses in the

At Haran, just as in the past, the family sleeps all together under a cone-shaped roof.

tiny village of Haran while the guardians of their sheep and goats move about with their flocks, and every two or three days have to take down and put up their black goatskin tents.

The architecture of Haran, as it was known to Abraham and to Jacob after him, has scarcely evolved at all. At the foot of the fortress, nowadays in ruins, there huddled a curious collection of houses; each was shaped like a sugar loaf and contained only one room. They were built of flat stones, placed one on top of the other without cement, and without the support of beams, since in this region trees were absolutely unknown. The only light which filtered into the house was obtained through a hole in the apex of the cone.

We may well believe that Jacob was received by his uncle in one of these curious dwellings. There was little furniture: on the beaten earth floor a few leather or woollen mats were spread; in a corner there stood perhaps a chest. And as the sun was already low on the horizon one or two lamps would have been lighted, simple earthenware vessels, whose rims at one place had been pinched together to form a rudimentary spout; in the oil contained in the lamps floated a flax wick which needed trimming fairly frequently.

Laban and his sons squatted down on a mat in front of Jacob. After the usual lengthy exchange of compliments Laban asked Jacob to tell the story of his adventures. Soon we shall get to know Laban better, for he too is quite a character. Many were his protestations of friendship and devotedness towards his kinsman: *'Truly,'* he said, *'you are my bone and flesh.'* It would be misleading to emphasize all this unduly. In the house at Haran, then, they celebrated Jacob's arrival for a month.

Jacob's service for his wife

More serious matters now claimed their attention. *'Because you are my kinsman,'* Laban said to Jacob, *'are you to work for me without payment? Tell me what wages you want'* (Gen. 29: 15). In addition to several sons, Laban had two daughters. Leah, the elder, was rather unpleasing in appearance and there was no *sparkle in her eyes*. Jacob found her unattractive. The younger, Rachel (*rahel,* a sheep), on the other hand, *was shapely and beautiful* Genesis is careful to inform us. It was obvious that Jacob had fallen in love with Rachel directly he saw her for the first time at the well. Since he had come to the Land of the Fathers to find a wife among the Arameans of pure stock (at least that was one of the reasons for his journey) why should he not ask Laban to give him Rachel for his bride? In addition, according to the custom of the time, his position as first cousin gave him a preferential advantage over any other claimant.[11] But Jacob had left the Hebrew camp at Beersheba owning nothing but his shepherd's staff, and he was certainly unable to pay the traditional *mohar*, a word often translated as 'dowry' or 'purchase price of a wife'.

Details of the mohar

Mesopotamian law fixed the amount at fifty shekels of

[11] In the ancient East (as even today among certain Arab tribes) a match between cousins was regarded as very desirable, for in this way the purity of the 'blood' of the line would be preserved. We have already encountered an example of this custom with the marriage of Isaac and Rebekah (see genealogical table, p. 46). Subsequently, the Bible furnishes several examples of this traditional custom. Thus the parents and grandparents of Moses were nephew and aunt, the latter being the father's sister (Exod. 6: 16, 18, 20; Num. 26: 59). Later still at the time of the Kings we find Rehoboam, Solomon's son, marrying Maacah, Absolom's daughter; now Solomon and Absolom were brothers, though not by the same mother, it is true.

silver.[12] But in certain cases payment in precious metal could be replaced by giving service, a practice which some historians regard as a more ancient institution than paying for a wife. In this case the young man offered to work for his father-in-law to be (or his legal representative) for nothing, so that at the end of the contract of service he could obtain the bride he desired.

'I will work for you seven years to win your younger daughter Rachel,' said Jacob. The bargain pleased Laban, and he replied: *'It is better for me to give her to you than to a stranger; stay with me.'*

The hard life of an oriental shepherd

It was certainly no sinecure looking after large flocks of sheep and goats in the open country of the Near East. As a rule the grass was thin and cropped short. As they went along the beasts grazed; from morning to night they lost not one minute, as they went slowly forward over the grass. Great expanses of pasture were consequently needed and those in charge of the flocks had to keep at a certain distance from each other. The shepherd of each flock was thus condemned to almost complete solitude. It was only in the evening at the local well that men were together for a short time.

Throughout the day watch could not be relaxed for a moment. If an animal wandered away, it had to be found and brought back; if one fell in a ravine it had to be pulled out. A sheep broke a leg, another was sick; the shepherd had to turn himself into bonesetter or veterinary surgeon. At lambing time there were innumerable duties to perform in caring for the ewes.

[12] Cf. Deut. 22: 29: the man who is convicted of seducing a young woman who is not yet betrothed must give the girl's father fifty silver shekels. There is an almost identical provision in Exod. 22: 15. The exact equivalent weight of a shekel is disputed. The *Jerusalem Bible* estimates it as 0·39 ozs or 0·0114 kilograms.

When night fell they had to be even more watchful: wolves, foxes, bears, even lions in certain parts, would prowl round the sleeping flocks. With the help of half-wild watchdogs the shepherd made continual rounds of the flocks and it was by no means rare for him to have to fight off the marauders. And then there were the human thieves as well who were certainly no less formidable.

The animals entrusted to the shepherd's care were counted and he remained responsible for them to his master. Both Sumerian and Semitic legislation agreed on this point. 'If a lion kills a beast in a sheepfold,' the Code of Hammurabi lays down, 'the owner of the sheepfold shall be responsible for the damage,' in other words, the shepherd was exonerated. The Hebrew law contains the following prescriptions: 'If the animal has been stolen from him [the shepherd], he must make restitution to the owner. If it has been savaged by wild beasts, he must bring the savaged remains of the animal as evidence, and he shall not be obliged to give compensation.'

One day when argument between Laban and Jacob grew heated the latter enumerated his grievances. He gave a graphic account of his activities which enables us to obtain a fairly close idea of his hard life as a shepherd. *'Your ewes and your she-goats have not miscarried'* [an expressive way of emphasizing that they had received all necessary care at lambing or kidding] *'and I have eaten none of the rams from your flock. As for those mauled by wild beasts, I have never brought them back'* [the legislative texts quoted above stated that the shepherd had the right to show proof of the fact and was thus freed from responsibility to make good the loss], *'but have borne the loss myself; you claimed them from me, whether I was robbed by day or robbed by night.'* [Here the argument was specious: with thefts in the proper sense of the term it was the shepherd's responsibility to track down the thieves or prevent them; he was responsible for everything that he allowed to be stolen.] *'In the daytime the heat has consumed me, and at night the cold has gnawed me, and sleep has fled from my eyes. . . . God has seen my weariness and the work done by my hands.'* Seven years of this hard life had been Jacob's, but he was working to win Rachel. And these seven years, Genesis tells us poetically, *seemed to him like a few days because he loved her so much*.

Set a thief to catch a thief

Jacob was now in a position to claim his wages from Laban; by his work he had paid off in some sort the dowry required of the bridegroom. *'My time is finished,'* he told his uncle. It was a splendid wedding. There was no religious ceremony at all at the time of the patriarchs. The chieftains of the neighbouring clans were invited for the celebrations and the banquetting continued for a whole week. On the first night the young wife, duly veiled, was taken to her husband's tent. All this followed the rites of the nomadic Semites.

Hitherto, Jacob seems to have acted on the principle of tricking others, but in uncle Laban he appears to have found one more cunning than himself. On the morning after the first wedding night, at daybreak, Jacob was astounded to find that it was not his beloved Rachel who had been brought into him but her elder sister Leah. The previous evening the veil covering her face had enabled Laban to play this trick, but at first light Jacob discovered how he had been made a fool of. There followed a stormy scene with his uncle. *'What is this you have done to me?'* demanded Jacob. *'Did I not work for you to win Rachel? Why then have you tricked me?'*

In an argument Laban could hold his own with anyone. *'It is not the custom in our country,'* he replied, *'to give the younger daughter before the elder.'* And he went on to offer Jacob another arrangement: *'Finish this marriage week and I will give you the other one too in return for your working with me another seven years.'* The bargain was concluded on the spot.

Laban had already given Leah a slave-girl named Zilpah. To Rachel on her wedding day he gave a slave-girl whose name was Bilhah. Both slaves were destined to play an important part in the development of the genealogical tree of Israel, since they soon became, quite legally, Jacob's concubines. Two wives and two concubines. Now Jacob *loved Rachel more than Leah*. We know what to expect. One master with four wives, one of whom was the favourite. Trouble was obviously looming.

The sons of Jacob

So far Jacob had been obliged to remain with his uncle for 'twice seven years'[13] to pay off the dowry (*mohar*) of his two wives, Leah and Rachel. Once free from this debt he remained six more years at Paddan-aram, according to Genesis, but now he was working on his own account. He needed to acquire wealth so that before very long he could return honourably to his father's camp in the Negeb.

Also, soon Jacob was to have twelve[14] sons, a symbolic figure which the scribes responsible for the biblical text were fond of emphasizing. We have already

[13] Seven years. This is a figure which recurs over and over again in the history of the Hebrews. It is used to indicate the completion of a perfect cycle. As for the three periods (amounting in all to twenty years) that Jacob spent with Laban it is better to regard them numerically in a general sense, and not give them their precise meaning.

[14] At the end of his period at Paddan-aram Jacob had still only eleven sons. The twelfth, Benjamin, was to be born to Rachel when the caravan, having left the region of the Euphrates, had penetrated into the land of Canaan and was on its way to the Negeb.

seen that Ishmael (the son of Abraham and Hagar the slave-girl) had twelve sons. In the institutions, in certain ritual descriptions and in a great number of narratives of the Old Testament, the figure twelve appears with particular emphasis. In fact twelve also was the sign of fullness. Thus to the twelve prophets of the Old Law there correspond the twelve apostles whom Jesus gathered round him.

Jacob, then, was to be father of twelve sons — who were to take their place in the history of Israel, not on account of their special worth but because each of them, after becoming the head of one of the twelve tribes of Israel, was to leave his name to one of these tribes which were destined to great political significance.

One chapter of Genesis describes with much picturesque detail how the names of the twelve sons were chosen. The oriental is intensely interested in everything concerning the genealogy of his important ancestors. But this passage might well remain incomprehensible without at this point some historical explanation.

In antiquity there were no family names. What we nowadays call Christian name or forename (a name chosen according to family tradition or the whim of the parents) must be regarded rather, at the period with which we are concerned, as a sort of nickname.

The eastern surname, bestowed on an individual at the moment of birth, as a general rule has nothing in common with the family name of western civilization which enables the complexities of the family tree to be more easily resolved. The purpose of the Semitic name is both social and religious and its object is to show the underlying nature of its bearer. It cannot be interchangeable. When a man is called by his name all the psychic powers of this name are set in motion; it has a real meaning. Hence its importance. Usually it was the mother who gave the name (at least in ancient times) at the birth of the child.

With this in mind we shall be in a better position to appreciate the social and religious thought governing the attribution of the names of Jacob's sons. For the birth of these twelve children was to be marked by many incidents; all this to the great satisfaction of the story-tellers and to the repeated joy of their audiences, not least because all these names in one way or another could be explained by means of puns.

Leah had been received somewhat coldly by her husband. To console her for this trial of her affections Yahweh was to make her fruitful while Jacob's beloved Rachel remained, for the time being at least, without children. This was hardly calculated to make for a peaceful family life.

Leah gave birth to her first son whom she called Reuben (*Ra'ah be'onyi*, 'he has seen my distress') and she added, *'now my husband will love me'*. So at least she hoped. She then produced a second son whom she called Simeon (*shama'*, 'he has heard'), meaning *Yahweh has heard that I was neglected, so he has given me this one too*. Leah had a third son. *'This time,'* she said, *'my husband will be united to me, for I have now borne three sons to him'* and so she named the child Levi (*yillaweh*, 'he will cling'). The fourth son was called Judah (*odeh*, 'I will praise').

In the circumstances Rachel's despair can be understood. In her distress she appealed to her husband, *'Give me children, or I shall die!'* Jacob reproved her angrily: *'Am I in God's place? It is he who has refused you motherhood.'* Rachel decided therefore to make use of the perfectly legal Sumerian practice which was adopted by Sarah when she was barren. Rachel gave Jacob her slave-girl Bilhah, who in due time gave birth to a son 'on the knees of her mistress' and thenceforward the child was regarded as Rachel's. *Then Rachel said, 'God has done me justice; yes, he has heard my prayer and given me a son.'* Thereupon she named him Dan (*dananni,* 'he has done justice to me').

After this success Rachel decided to repeat it; she continued to be a mother, through the agency of Bilhah, who gave her a second son. *'I have fought God's fight with my sister,'* announced Rachel, *'and I have won.'* And so she named him Naphtali (*niphtalti,* 'I have fought').

All this time Leah, who with four sons, was well in advance of her sister, produced no more. But she took care not to allow herself to be beaten by Rachel in this curious competition. Her father Laban had given her also as a wedding present the slave-girl Zilpah. She too must enter the family circle. There followed another birth according to the Sumerian pattern. To the son who was born thus Leah gave the name Gad (*gad,* 'good luck'). Once more Zilpah bore a son, causing Leah to utter a cry of victory, *'What happiness! Women will call me happy!'* So she named him Asher (*'osheri,* 'my happiness' and *'ishsheruni,* 'they will count me happy').

It was now Leah's turn to give birth – in person this time. *'God has paid me my wages,'* she exclaimed. This fifth son was Issachar (*sakar,* 'he has hired' and *sakar,* 'wages'). When she gave birth to a sixth son, Zebulun (*yizbeleni,* 'he will respect me') she hoped that at last Jacob would give her the honour due to her. After all these sons Leah produced a daughter, Dinah, who later on was to play a part in the troubles of the clan.

Then God remembered Rachel. He heard her prayers and she gave birth to a son. This was the famous Joseph who one day was to summon all his brothers to Egypt where he had become a high official. The birth of this

Rachel must have looked like this.

ardently desired child caused Rachel to exclaim, *'God has taken away my shame!'* and she added a prayer that Yahweh would give her another son. There was a double pun here: *'asaph,* meaning 'he has taken away' and *yoseph,* 'may he add', foretelling the future birth of Benjamin.

In all these rather forced etymologies there appears an element of popular entertainment. The Yahwistic tradition clearly predominates here. Down the ages the wandering shepherds endeavoured to explain by means of phonetic approximations, which seem very fanciful to us, the names of the eponymous heroes of Israel, the leaders of the Twelve Tribes.

How Jacob became rich

Laban had tricked Jacob into taking a wife whom he did not want. According to the mentality of the Hebrew nomads it was quite normal for Jacob to seize the first occasion for his revenge. It was a primitive form of morality which still stood in need of evolution. Joseph the eleventh son had just been born at this time. Jacob took the opportunity to tell Laban of his desire to leave this region of the Euphrates and to return with his wives and children to his native Negeb. But Laban, not wishing to lose a valuable associate, insisted on his nephew's remaining in his service. Jacob therefore laid down his terms.

They were rather surprising. In addition, the passage which tells us of them contains many glosses [15] which,

[15] 'Glosses' are the explanatory notes which certain readers of ancient manuscripts added in the margins of ancient manuscripts or else between the lines to clarify the text by a phrase or additional statement. Most of the ancient codices which have survived provide proof of this custom. Subsequently, when a scribe copied a document enriched with glosses he often thought it right to incorporate these notes in the original text. These additions are sometimes improvements but can also on occasion prove ill-advised. Fortunately modern philologists usually succeed in detecting the gloss because in style or vocabulary it differs from the context.

for once, instead of helping us to understand, complicate the facts of the case. The various articles of the contract are not put before us very clearly, but we can try to discover their meaning.

In the first place, it should be realized that in the pastures of the Near East the smaller livestock is usually uniform in colour; the goats are usually completely black and the sheep a dirty white. There are few black sheep and still fewer white-spotted goats.

With this in mind we can examine the terms of the bargain offered by Jacob to his uncle. As in the past, Jacob would continue to look after Laban's flocks in the pastureland of Paddan-aram, but after the breeding period, that is at the end of spring, a division would be made: all the animals of a single colour would belong to Laban; those of two colours, the exceptions, would be Jacob's; they would constitute his wages. Laban was sure that he had a good bargain and hastened to agree.

Obviously he did not realize that he was dealing with an astute young man. Jacob then carried out some very curious operations. In front of the troughs (when the flocks were taken to drink was the time when the males covered the females) he placed branches of trees from which the bark had been partially removed so that they appeared to the eye as having white and green stripes. Since the sight of these stripes influenced the morphological character of the embryo Jacob soon succeeded in obtaining a herd of goats which was almost completely spotted. He took care that the white sheep should mate while they were looking at a herd of black goats. Black lambs were the result. Of course, modern zoologists and specialists in genetics would certainly not accept these explanations.

It hardly needs mentioning that Jacob only made use of sturdy animals. The weaker ones did not undergo any special treatment; on this account they kept their original colours and their offspring formed Laban's share. Something had to be kept for him after all. But Jacob with his original methods of selection gradually built up large flocks of striped, spotted or abnormally coloured sheep and goats.

Jacob's unexpected success caused Laban's sons to murmur. *'Jacob,'* they were saying among themselves, *'has taken everything that belonged to our father; it is at our father's expense that he has acquired all this wealth.'* In the circumstances Laban thought it advisable to change the terms of the contract; as many as ten times, Jacob informs us. But, as Genesis explains, Yahweh was protecting Jacob, although, as we have seen, he appeared well able to look after his own interests.

If Laban required as his share all the spotted animals the kids and lambs were all of one colour; if the following year he claimed all the animals of one colour those which were born were all speckled. Thus gradually Jacob became the owner of considerable livestock. He had even been able to acquire tents, slaves and even camels, by the sale of the wool from his sheep. Between uncle and nephew the situation grew increasingly tense.

In such circumstances it might have been prudent to seize the first opportunity of leaving the country. But suddenly amidst these family differences Yahweh made his voice heard. It might be thought that so far he had left the man of his choice very much to his own devices. But in no way had he abandoned him to his fate. The time had now come for Yahweh to appear, to speak, to command. Characteristically, it was during a dream that he manifested himself to Jacob: *'I am the God of Bethel,'* he announced, *'where you poured oil on a monument, and where you made a vow to me.'*

Had Jacob forgotten Bethel? Yahweh fully intended

to make his own man of his keen-witted shepherd, although he was for the time being deeply involved in material cares, to transform him spiritually and to entrust him with a mission. *'I am the God of Bethel. . . . Now get ready to leave this country and return to the land of your birth.'*

Jacob leaves the land of the Fathers

Jacob has already been likened to a Mazarin of the Old Testament. He was no lover of open hostilities and in all circumstances tried to solve by peaceful methods the most delicate problems; by means of a calm and thoughtful discussion he was almost always sure to emerge unscathed from a difficult situation, even if he had not always right on his side. And it was thus he acted when he left Haran.

Jacob holds a family council

From certain indications to be mentioned shortly, it seems probable that Jacob's wives and young children lived at Haran itself in the curious houses with conical roofs, while he as chief shepherd with the other shepherds followed the flocks from pasture to pasture on the grassy plain. One morning he returned to the gate of the city with his flocks, his tents, his servants and slaves. In reality Jacob had chosen his time, for then Laban was three days' journey from the city where he was supervising the shearing of a flock. We know that Jacob had no taste for a dispute, and for the moment his position was without danger.

At once he called a sort of family council with his two legitimate wives, Leah and Rachel. He explained to them his grievances against their father Laban, and recalled the very considerable hard work that he had had to do for the chieftain of the tribe. He described the threatening attitude that Laban's sons were beginning to adopt as his own flocks increased in number. His success, he explained, was due to the protection of Yahweh who had fortunately lent his aid in the struggle against the greed and bad faith of Laban. After these explanations he told them that Yahweh, the God of Abraham and Isaac, had just commanded him to return to the camp in the Negeb.

The two wives, who it must be admitted seemed to have no great feeling for their father, agreed with their husband. It was a family scene in the best tradition. So far, observed Leah and Rachel, their father had entirely failed to give them *'any share . . . in the inheritance of* [their] *father's house'*. Quite bluntly they expressed their bitterness: *'Does he not treat us as foreigners, for he has sold us and gone on to use up all our money.'*

The argument was perhaps a little exaggerated. The two sisters were alluding to the *mohar,* a part of which was usually kept for the wife, and of course niggardly Laban had taken good care to do nothing of the sort. Hence the women's anger. For once Leah and Rachel seemed to be in complete agreement. *'So do all that God has told you,'* they concluded.

Without delay the secret move was carried out. Women and children took their places in the covered saddles which were strapped to the camels. The scanty furniture was quickly loaded. The camping equipment was loaded on to donkeys. Jacob's shepherds, servants and slaves did their best to take up positions all round their master's huge flocks, and in a tremendous cloud of dust the long caravan set off.

Before leaving, Rachel succeeded in obtaining entry into Laban's house, which was probably quite near. There she managed to lay hands on her father's *teraphim.* According to the small amount of information which we possess about these objects of worship it seems that they can be regarded, at least in the present case, as the domestic idols, the tutelary deities of the family. Excavations in Palestine have brought to light a certain number of these figurines which were venerated by the adherents of the polytheistic religions. They seem to have been used on occasion for certain magical activities connected with divination. In addition the *teraphim* constituted a title to the inheritance; we can understand in consequence the gravity of Rachel's act.

The journey went on and on. After fording the Euphrates the caravan turned south, making for Mount Gilead, the Transjordanian massif on the left bank of the Jordan and therefore to the south-east of the Lake of Gennesaret. It was well-wooded country and also rich in fine pastureland.

Laban pursues Jacob

Three days after Jacob's departure Laban was informed of his nephew's rather unusual behaviour. The shearing was abandoned, and taking with him some of his sons, Laban set off in pursuit of the fugitive.

We know that Laban was a man of irascible temperament, so that a scene of some violence might be expected when the two men came face to face. In fact the encounter between them was far from assuming the dramatic character which might at first have been feared. Moreover, Genesis tells us that that night *God* [but not the God of Laban] *came by night in a dream to Laban and said to him, 'On no account say anything whatever to Jacob'*. For a polytheist any deity, even a foreign one, is to be treated with awe and reverence. Laban made up his mind to obey the order which had thus been given to him. That, of course, did not prevent a man of his quick temper from telling his nephew exactly what he thought, but matters never went to the extremes which might have been feared.

Directly Laban and Jacob met discussion was vehement and wide ranging. Laban's reproaches of Jacob were not exactly groundless: *'Why did you flee in secret, stealing away without letting me know so that I could send you on your way rejoicing, with music of tambourines and lyres? You did not even let me kiss my sons [grandsons] and daughters. You have behaved like a fool'* (Gen. 31: 27–9). Crestfallen, Jacob could only reply, *'I was afraid'*.

Laban had not finished. *'Why,'* he demanded, *'did you steal my gods?'* He was referring to the *teraphim*. Jacob, who knew nothing of Rachel's theft, declared his total ignorance of the matter. And he suggested that his uncle should set about a methodical search of all the baggage; he promised that the culprit would not remain alive. First Leah's tent was inspected and then that of the two slave-girls. There now remained Rachel's tent. She had hidden the idols in the litter which, when unloaded from the camel, was placed in the shelter of the tent while the caravan was halted. Rachel was sitting on the litter. *'Do not look angry, my Lord, because I cannot rise in your presence, for I am as women are from time to time.'* Among all the Semites a woman during her period was regarded as unclean and everything that she touched became defiled by the mere contact. We can understand why Laban did not search the litter; he even took care to leave the tent as soon as possible.

This was the cue for Jacob, with his usual guile, to launch into a vehement tirade, shouting out that he had been accused unjustly, calling to witness all those present at the insult done to him. It formed a good opportunity for him also to enumerate all the work that he had done for a very long time for a mere pittance:

'These twenty years I have been in your house; fourteen years I have worked for you for your two daughters, and six years for your flocks. . . . If the God of my father, the God of Abraham, the Kinsman of Isaac, had not been with me, you would have sent me away empty-handed.'

Jacob was a diplomat of the first order; in a reasoned argument his native subtlety gave him the advantage.

A treaty between Jacob and Laban

Laban made up his mind. *'Come now,'* he said, *'let us make a covenant, you and I.'* There then followed a strange ceremony, very properly of a religious nature, by which each contracting party solemnly undertook to abide by the articles of the treaty. Despite the glosses, which have somewhat obscured the meaning of the passage, we can attempt to reconstruct the scene.

First those taking part set about collecting medium-sized stones and heaping them up to make a cairn. Beside this was set a raised stone (*massebah*), that is, a stele. On the heap of stones the two contracting parties took a meal together. From earliest antiquity bread and wine, eaten and drunk together, establish bonds of lasting friendship, at least in principle. A characteristic example of this has already been encountered at the meeting of Abraham and Melchizedek, who also partook of bread and wine together. We are reminded here of the symbolism of the Eucharist, a meal taken in common, though of course of spiritual food. And the centuries-old tradition of the bonds established by partaking together of the same meal was not to be lost in east or west. Etymologically the English word *companion* is derived from *companis,* 'he with whom bread has been shared'.

This cairn, which had now become a sacred place, Laban named in his Aramaic language *Jegar-sahadutha* and Jacob, in ancient Hebrew, *Galeed.* The two terms can be translated in identical fashion: 'cairn of witness'. Obviously, we are to expect the formulation of a ritual pledge or undertaking. Laban said: *'May this cairn be a witness between us today . . . when we are no longer in sight of each other.'* Laban thereupon put forward two requests: Jacob was not to illtreat Leah and Rachel; on the other hand he was not to take any further wives. This was the strictly family side of the business.

But the very important matter of pastoral boundaries remained to be settled. Laban, who certainly seems to have led the discussions, put forward a further proposal. He was by no means anxious, and we can understand his reluctance, to see his nephew returning one day with even more numerous flocks to the pastures of Paddan-aram. He wanted Jacob to go back to the Negeb and stay there. *'Here,'* said Laban, *'is this cairn I have thrown up between us, and here is the monument. This cairn is a witness, and the monument bears witness: I must not pass this cairn to attack you, and you must not pass this cairn and this monument to attack me.'* In some way it was a boundary post.

The political agreement was very properly ratified by a solemn undertaking in which the deity of each party was called to witness. Jacob swore by his God, *the Kinsman of his father Isaac,* and Laban by the God of Nahor (Nahor, it will be remembered, was Abraham's brother; and Nahor, and indeed his whole clan, had remained faithful to the Semitic and Sumerian deities).

The religious ceremony did not end there. As patriarch, the head of the tribe, Jacob proceeded to offer a sacrifice to Yahweh on the mountain; he took care to invite all *his brothers,* that is, all the men present, including those who had followed Laban on his expedition. Once more there was a meal taken together. And the group passed the night on the mountain.

Next morning they parted company. Laban kissed his daughters and grandsons and blessed them. Then he returned home to the Land of the Fathers. Jacob, freed at last from all fear of his uncle, set off for the south towards the Jabbok, a tributary of the Jordan which he expected to be able to ford, and also the Jordan itself, and so enter the land of Canaan. One chapter of Jacob's story was over.

Across the ford of the Jabbok

Jacob moved forward, following his sheep which, as they went along cropped the fine pasture of Transjordania. And so no one hurried, neither flocks nor shepherds. Jacob himself was glad at last to be on the road taking him back to his father's tents, but he felt a little anxious; on arrival in the Negeb, perhaps even beforehand, he had an old account to settle with his brother Esau, the fiery and brutal hunter. It was not a pleasant prospect.

Slowly then they advanced towards the south. Jacob had decided that the caravan would ford the Jabbok (the modern *Nahr ez-Zerqa,* one of the most important rivers of Transjordania, which it divides into almost equal parts). After this difficult operation they were to go on towards the Jordan which, too, they would ford. And so the clan would come to the land of Canaan. Immediately on entering the Promised Land Jacob intended to establish his camp at Bethel, at the place where Yahweh had appeared to him in a dream when, as a poor shepherd with no flocks, he was journeying to Haran.

Fording the Jabbok and settling at Bethel form two decisive moments in the spiritual transformation of the Patriarch Jacob.

At Mahanaim, a warning from God

Since Jacob's first stay at Bethel and the famous dream

of the 'ladder', during which Yahweh had renewed to him the terms of the promise already made to Abraham and Isaac, it does not seem that Yahweh had spoken to Jacob again. During his long exile at Paddan-aram Jacob appears only to have received very rare messages confined to his material interests, such as the assurance of numerous descendants (a fixed idea with all Semitic peoples), advice on increasing the amount of his livestock (the desire for wealth being firmly established in the hearts of most men), and the organization of a supernatural form of defence against certain hostile forces. In all this we encounter a very primitive faith in which the function of the tribal god is to protect his devotee. It is a rather down-to-earth form of religion whose existence has been confirmed by the results of excavations in the archaeological strata corresponding with this period.

But Genesis is not concerned to show us the general form taken by the civilizations which followed each other in Canaan. Its task rather is to inform us about the missions entrusted to certain men chosen by God to contribute to the spiritual evolution of humanity. Hitherto, Jacob the son of Isaac has certainly appeared to us as a Semitic shepherd endowed with nimble wits, but not, it would seem, very open to inspiration from God; in addition, his moral level was not very high. Yet twenty years previously at Bethel Yahweh chose this Hebrew shepherd to carry out part of the divine plan. The God of Abraham bided his time, but that time was now soon to come.

Jacob was going on his way, we are told in Genesis, when *angels of God met him, and on seeing them he said, 'This is God's camp,'* and he named the place *Mahanaim*. Mahanaim is the plural (or rather the dual, as the Hebrew grammarians say) of *Mahaneh,* camp. It is a term that can be explained in two ways, historically and symbolically.

Historically: we shall see shortly that Jacob was in a very critical situation: Esau with his armed men was on his way to meet Jacob and a confrontation was inevitable. As a good tactician he decided to split up the people and flocks with him into two companies; if one was captured, the other would escape. This was no doubt the reason for the name given to this locality; at a later date the Transjordanian city Mahanaim was to be established here; it was to be called on to play a part in the history of Israel (2 Sam. 2: 8; 17: 24; 1 Kings 4: 14).

Symbolically this unexpected appearance of the 'angels' (a reminder of the famous 'ladder') might be regarded as a warning from Yahweh announcing that he intended to take up again the dialogue previously begun at Bethel. So we have a material and a religious explanation which are in no way contradictory.

Exchange of messages between Jacob and Esau

Jacob as a sensible man was going to try to find a compromise which would settle once and for all the difference between him and his brother Esau over the question of the inheritance. As he returned from Haran, Jacob hardly felt that he could push on peacefully into the land of Canaan with his fat flocks if Esau maintained his position and was still of a mind to kill his brother to satisfy his thirst for vengeance. It was not, however, by force of arms but by clever negotiation that Jacob intended to settle the matter.

He was careful not to make contact with Esau personally; at the outset, at least, he preferred to act through intermediaries. The first messengers were instructed to inform Esau that Jacob was on his way back from

Laban's house with *oxen, beasts of burden and flocks, and men and women slaves* and that he hoped to win approval in the eyes of Esau. Having carried out their mission the messengers returned quickly to Jacob with the alarming news that Esau was on his way to meet him at the head of four hundred armed men.

Jacob sought a hasty solution: he would try to appease Esau's anger by loading him with gifts. This was his plan. A herd of *two hundred she-goats and twenty he-goats, two hundred ewes and twenty rams, thirty camels in milk with their calves, forty cows and ten bulls, twenty she-asses and ten donkeys* was despatched to Esau. To the servants in charge of these animals he gave the following orders: *'When my brother meets you and asks, "To whom do you belong? Where are you going? Whose are the animals that you are driving?"* [traditional questions asked of strangers on the steppes] *you will answer, "To your servant Jacob. They are a gift sent to my lord Esau. Jacob himself is following".'* This was sure to produce a certain effect. But it was only intended as a beginning.

A short distance behind the first drove, followed a second made up in the same way: she-goats and he-goats, ewes and rams, camels with their calves, cows and bulls, she-asses and donkeys. Esau would certainly question the servant in charge of the drove; he was to answer in exactly the same terms as the first. Shortly afterwards came a third drove with similar instructions. All three were told to conclude their explanations with the remark, *'Yes, your servant Jacob himself is following'.* That, then, was the carefully laid plan, for in this way Jacob thought *'I shall conciliate him by sending a gift in advance; so when I come face to face with him he may perhaps receive me favourably.'*

As the three droves set off one after the other Jacob,

still at Mahanaim, made a fervent prayer to Yahweh; it was a moving, almost pathetic petition couched in terms that so far could hardly have been expected of Jacob. There were, so to say, four movements. Firstly, there was the reminder of his act of obedience: *'When I was at Paddan-aram you told me to return to my country; I have carried out your order.'* Then, an act of humility (as there should be in every prayer): *'I am unworthy of all the kindness and goodness you have shown your servant.'* Thirdly, there was the feeling of panic in the face of imminent danger. He told Yahweh that formerly he had only his staff when he crossed the Jordan there, and now he was rich and with his flocks he could form two companies or camps (*mahanaim*). But this wealth so patiently acquired would be reduced to nothing if his brother was filled with anger against him. *'Lord, save me from the clutches of my brother, I am afraid of him.'* Fear – that is characteristic of Jacob. In conclusion, there was an appeal for mercy, by invoking the solemn Promise already made on different occasions to his grandfather Abraham, to his father Isaac and even to the grandson, Jacob himself.

Shortly there was to occur one of those profound transformations of which the Bible (and on occasion modern religious history) often provides examples, when God, working on the souls of men who seem ill-prepared, for such an assault, makes them his own and incorporates them in his constructive plan.

Jacob wrestles with God

With the fording of the Jabbok we come to one of the most enigmatic accounts in Genesis. So far it has been possible to avoid long biblical quotations, but here it will be necessary to reproduce a sequence of verses which Old Testament scholars usually group together under the somewhat dramatic title of 'the struggle or fight with God'. After this an attempt will be made to examine the terms and provide the necessary explanations.

Jacob had just despatched the three droves to Esau in the hope of appeasing the anger which might still be in his heart. *Jacob passed that night there,* that is, at Mahanaim. *That same night he rose, and taking his two wives and his two slave-girls* [concubines] *and his eleven children he crossed the ford of the Jabbok. He took them and sent them across the stream and sent all his possessions over too. And Jacob was left alone. And there was one that wrestled* [another play on words: *ye'abeq,* 'wrestled', in conjunction with the name of the river] *with him until daybreak who, seeing that he could not master him, struck him in the socket of the hip, and Jacob's hip was dislocated as he wrestled with him. He said, 'Let me go, for day is breaking.' But Jacob answered, 'I will not let you go unless you bless me.' He then asked, 'What is your name?' 'Jacob,' he replied. He said, 'Your name shall no longer be Jacob, but Israel, because you have been strong against God, you shall prevail against men.' Jacob then made this request, 'I beg you, tell me your name,' but he replied, 'Why do you ask my name?' And he blessed him there.*

Jacob named the place Peniel, 'Because I have seen God face to face,' he said, 'and I have survived.' The sun rose as he left Peniel, limping because of his hip. That is the reason why to this day the Israelites do not eat the sciatic nerve which is in the socket of the hip; because he had struck Jacob in the socket of the hip on the sciatic nerve (Gen. 32: 23–33).

Jacob's physical combat

The caravan had taken advantage of the cool of the evening to ford the Jabbok. Most probably they had chosen the season when the waters were low, but the operation remained difficult nonetheless and quite dangerous for the animals of the flock. The patriarch who was directing the crossing in person was the last to leave the river bank, but just at the moment when he was thus alone on the other side of the river he was attacked by a mysterious person (literally, *'ish,* 'someone') and was obliged to wrestle with him until dawn. It was a hand-to-hand struggle whose strange ups and downs always impress the reader of this passage of the Bible. We can now examine this account more closely.

The episode falls naturally into three phases: by a skilful hold his opponent immobilized Jacob by a blow on the sciatic nerve in his hip; Jacob's name was changed to Israel; Jacob, who finally discovered the identity of his assailant, declared that he has seen God face to face.

The sciatic nerve. Because he could not master Jacob, Yahweh struck Jacob on the hip to put him out of action. It appears that from this moment Jacob was to limp for the rest of his life. In addition, Genesis adds, in memory of the combat waged by their great ancestor the Israelites never ate the sciatic nerve of the wild or domestic animals which they killed. This dietary prohibition appears here in the Bible for the first and last time. It does not seem that the Jews ever observed it, but it is found elsewhere than in Israel; some scholars believe that sometimes in the East the sciatic nerve is regarded as the seat of the reproductive powers.

The change of name. This is characteristic of the nomadic period. For the name designates the inner nature of a person, so that to know this name means knowing the person and also gives a certain power over him. We have already seen how Yahweh gave Abram a new name, Abraham, and at the same time his wife Sarai became Sarah. In the ancient Near East a person made a sudden change of name, either on his own authority or, more frequently, on the orders of a supernatural power, in order to mark a new vocation, or to emphasize and in some sort explain a moral or social transformation. And so here we find Yahweh saying, *'Your name shall be no longer Jacob, but Israel; because you have been strong against God, you shall prevail against men'*.

About a thousand years after the fording of the Jabbok the prophet Hosea maked this comment, *'In maturity, he* [Jacob] *wrestled against God. He wrestled with the angel* [who here takes the place of God] *and beat him'* (Hos. 12: 4–5). The original reads that Jacob 'was strong against' God, and indeed this expression has almost something of a shocking implication: how can a human creature claim to 'beat' him who alone is almighty?

In fact this expression should be considered as a popular explanation, unconcerned with accuracy of terms, whose obvious purpose is to give cause for pride to the patriarch's descendants. The linguistic meaning of this expression is the root *sarah,* to be strong. But the nomad shepherds, and the scribes after them, no doubt, overlooked the fact that in a proper name composed of a verb and the term 'El (God) the latter must of necessity be the subject of the sentence. The modern school of Hebrew scholars has examined the problem and has come to the conclusion that the name Israel should be translated not by the expression 'strong against God' (which it is difficult to admit) but rather by the statement, which has a certain majesty, 'God is strong' or 'May God show his strength'.

This translation is far more satisfactory than the standard one, for it allows us to see how Yahweh manifests himself increasingly in Jacob's soul, hitherto plunged in darkness.

Jacob named the place Peniel [face of God], *'Because*

I have seen God face to face,' he said, *'and I have survived.'* The little village of Peniel is situated on the left bank of the Jabbok, near the ford over the river. It is to be identified with the modern Tulul edh-Dhahab, a double hill commanding the ford of the Jabbok. It is not entirely certain whether the centre was already in existence in Jacob's time.

Peniel (face of God). *'I have seen God face to face,'* exclaimed Jacob at the end of his nocturnal adventure, *'and I have survived'*. In the Bible the face of God is synonomous with God himself. The expression is used to refer to God's active presence and through it his protection. On his chosen ones God sometimes bestows the favour of direct knowledge. It must not be inferred from that that God is seen with the bodily eyes; what we are here concerned with is a mysterious but direct relationship between the invisible God and his creature. But it is rare for a human being to survive even a partial experience of this sort. Scripture warns us that we shall only see the face of God clearly in the next life. Jacob's astonishment can be understood at finding himself alive after this extraordinary experience.

At this point of the story it should be observed that at the strictly historical level its various elements taken as a whole seem questionable. And that is the view of the majority of biblical scholars. Nowadays, exegetes believe that the interest of the narrative is to be found, in accordance indeed with the intentions of the sacred writer, in its religious teaching. And it should not be forgotten that the author in ancient times, in order to record and explain Jacob's conversion, had at his disposal only a concrete vocabulary. Thus modern commentators are in general agreement that this hand-to-hand struggle of the two opponents should be regarded as a spiritual combat which took place in Jacob's heart. And this even if Jacob's lameness was due to an injury of the sciatic nerve, to be explained in another way.

Jacob's spiritual combat

Night fell on the banks of the Jabbok. We may also believe that Jacob's conscience had been concerned, and for sometime past, by the darkening forces of evil. Cunning and crafty as he was it seemed that he no longer felt at ease in this materialistic, suffocating universe in which he had enclosed himself.

Already at Bethel Jacob had been privileged to hear the word of God which had been full of encouragement and goodwill. In addition God had revealed the great mission awaiting him. Now at Bethel he did not understand, or did not want to understand, the spiritual meaning of the message addressed to him. He still remained at the level, which he felt to be safer, of human wisdom. Without rejecting the unexpected help offered by Yahweh, his acceptance of the fulfilment of the divine promises was conditional; he was certainly very cautious when dealing with the supernatural. Earthly good came first. During his sojourn in Paddan-aram, nonetheless, he did not forget Yahweh. A careful reading of the account of his life at this period shows in this still untutored soul the secret workings of divine grace. There are just a few indications, still infrequent, but worth pointing out. Thus at the end of his long service in the Land of the Fathers we observed him making a sort of primitive examination of conscience, in which he acknowledged that the God of Abraham, the one God of the Hebrew tribe, had protected him in a very special and effective way throughout his whole life as a shepherd. A little later, when in the highlands of Gilead Laban succeeded in overtaking him, he made no mystery of the favours and care lavished on him by Yahweh: *'If the God of my father,'* Jacob explained to his uncle, *'had not been with me, you would have sent me away empty-handed; but God has seen my weariness and the work done by my hands'* (Gen. 31: 42; cf. verse 7).

The modern reader will no doubt find some cause for astonishment at this sort of religion so closely bound up with a businesslike approach: what was promised has been received. Obviously we should like to discern a purer, more spontaneous impulse in the heart of the representative of the third generation of patriarchs, endowed with a mission by the one God. Jacob is still very close to the polytheistic mentality based on the idea of a gift for a gift: *'For my prayer to be heard I will sacrifice an animal on your altar',* or, again, *'I make this sacrifice to thank you for having answered my request, for having allowed the success of my plans'*. Any movement of real, deep love, seems entirely absent from the ceremony. The only concern was the ritual, that is, the correct pronouncing of the formulas.

And yet as the hours went by Jacob felt the onset of fearful anguish. The future was dark: it had been announced that Esau was on his way to Peniel, there would be heated argument and the accounts concerning the matter of the paternal blessing would have to be settled. As a way out of the difficulty Jacob was depending to some extent on his talents for manoeuvre and particularly on his skill in argument. Even so, he wondered whether these purely human methods would be enough.

So it was natural that in this predicament he should turn to Yahweh to implore his help. In fact at this dramatic turning point of his existence he recognized his own weakness. For the first time, it appears, there rose up from his heart a fervent and really humble prayer: *'O God of my father Abraham ... I am unworthy of all the kindness and goodness you have shown your servant ... I implore you save me from my brother's clutches, for I am afraid of him. ... It was you who said, "I will make you prosper". . .'*

But Yahweh, as we know, asks to be loved for his own sake; he requires the complete, whole-hearted adhesion of his faithful follower. At that time Jacob was still far from possessing Abraham's pure and lucid faith, or even Isaac's, which though less apparent was nonetheless sincere. With Jacob there was too much bargaining, too much wavering, and insufficient concern for the things of the spirit. What was still lacking in this man of materialist outlook whom Yahweh had chosen was about to be made good. The time seemed favourable for an infusion of grace.

Thus gradually we come to the incident often referred to as Jacob's struggle with God. It is a struggle that we have all experienced, indeed most men have gone through it. Jacob means us. The night at the Jabbok we have also experienced in our own souls, in the depths of our conscience by the resistance that we have offered to the Spirit of God.

Yahweh needed Jacob for the carrying out of the plan that the patriarch was shortly to bring to a successful conclusion. Jacob accepted his defeat willingly; henceforth his eyes were to be open to spiritual realities. Thus he agreed to let his vanquisher go, and on leaving him God gave him his blessing.[16]

The change of name was a symbol of conversion. By giving Jacob this new name God took possession of his

[16] In this chapter, which is difficult to explain adequately, I have followed Fr Tamisier, P.S.S. in his article 'L'Itinéraire spirituel de Jacob' in *Bible et Terre sainte*, no. 47, May 1962.

Jacob must have had features like this.

patriarch. In the future Jacob-Israel was to be animated with a real and living faith which by definition made him ready to carry out the will of God.

The two brothers meet

Meanwhile Esau at the head of his four hundred men was making progress and very shortly came in sight of Jacob's tents. On the latter's orders his whole household went out to meet the new arrival, and the order in which they went expressed fairly accurately the feelings of the head of the family. At the head walked the two concubines with their sons, then, after an interval came Leah (the less loved of the two wives) and her sons. Finally, after a further interval, followed Rachel, the woman who occupied first place in Jacob's heart, together with Joseph, her only son.

At the head of this frightened group walked Jacob; part ambassador, part suppliant, he went forward to meet his brother and bowed seven times to the ground before going up to him. It was an intentional exaggeration of the customary marks of respect. The Canaanite princes were accustomed to bow seven times before their overlords, but among' the Arameans one low bow was the usual rule. Probably Jacob thought it wise to appease Esau's anger by a somewhat exaggerated display of humility.

Esau-Edom, known as 'the red', whose skin was possibly not so thick as might be thought, ran to meet his younger brother, and affectionately lifted him to his feet. *He took him in his arms,* says Genesis, *and held him close and wept*. From that moment Jacob could feel that the family question was settled in his favour. Indeed everything seemed to succeed for him, and his confidence in Yahweh's protection must have become stronger.

Time moves slowly in the East, and the nomads were usually glad of an opportunity for an exchange of compliments. Esau, who must certainly have had a shrewd idea of the identity of the groups arranged in order behind his brother, asked who they were. *'The children,'* replied Jacob, *'whom God has bestowed on your servant.'* They were brought forward in order, the concubines with their sons first, and then the wives, all with much bowing low.

Esau seems to have decided to profit by the turn of events. With a certain ingenuousness he inquired, *'What was the meaning of all the company that I have met?'* The remark did not refer, as might be supposed, to the three droves sent at short intervals as gifts. Esau meant one of the two companies into which Jacob had divided his livestock; he had done so, it will be recalled, as a precautionary measure in case of an attack by Esau. *'What do you mean to do with all the livestock that I met?'* asked Esau craftily. The time had come, Jacob decided, to make some sacrifice to attain his ends. *'It is to win my lord's favour,'* he replied. As required by oriental good manners Esau refused, half-heartedly. Jacob, reading his thoughts, insisted. *'I came into your presence as into the presence of God, but you have received me kindly,'* he replied, meaning thereby that from the beginning of the meeting with his brother he had felt the same feeling of terror as when coming face to face with God. It was an excess of flattery but good policy. It was nonetheless true that Jacob had been very afraid. In the end Esau accepted the present. Jacob could reckon quite rightly that on a last analysis peace had not been bought at too dear a price.[17]

---

[17] On a rapid reading of the passage it might be thought that Esau had accepted, in the first place, the three droves sent to him by Jacob, and intended to appease his anger, and, secondly, the half of Jacob's flocks, which had been divided into two camps (*mahanaim*). In fact these two 'presents' should not be added to each other. The sending of the three droves belongs to the Yahwistic tradition, the gift of the 'second camp' to the Elohistic cycle. The scribe incorporated them both without making any distinction.

The brothers separate

We must not expect Jacob to have been immediately 'converted' at the ford of the Jabbok, with an abrupt change in the depths of his personality. He still remained a very 'careful' man. The ascent had been begun indeed but the patriarch was still at the bottom of the slope which he still had to climb by degrees.

Esau proposed to his brother that they should travel together to the land of Seir (that is one of the names of the region of Edom) where he had settled with his flocks.[18] Jacob declined. His herds and flocks, he explained, were made up for the most part of sheep and cows that had calved, *'If they were driven too hard, even for one day, the whole drove will die.'* And then there were young children in the caravan who could not push forward quickly. *'May it please my lord to go ahead of his servant. For my part, I will move at a slower pace, to suit the flock I am driving and the children, until I join my lord in Seir.'* Jacob must have felt it advisable not to strain the understanding between Esau and himself. Directly Esau had started Jacob set off in the opposite direction. He went towards Shechem.

Towards the Promised Land

In any case, after their recent tiring journeys, the beasts needed careful treatment. Thus soon after the two brothers had separated we find Jacob settling, almost as if permanently, a short distance from Peniel. In this grassy country, excellent for the raising of stock, the shepherds built themselves houses, though probably of a quite primitive and temporary kind. For the animals

---

[18] This is in accordance with the Yahwistic (J) and Elohistic (E) traditions. But according to the Priestly tradition (P) Esau was still living at Hebron with Isaac and did so until the return of Jacob. This point will be discussed at the appropriate time (see page 104).

shelters were put up made out of branches, hence the name of the place Succoth (a shelter of branches).

. After this pause in their travels which lasted perhaps for several years the caravan passed over the Jordan. At last they were setting foot in the land of Canaan, the Promised Land set apart by Yahweh as the patrimony of the Chosen People.

Jacob at Shechem, then at Bethel

For the polytheist Abraham, who in southern Mesopotamia 'had served other gods' belonging to Semitic and Sumerian pantheons, adhesion to the new faith revealed by Yahweh, the one God, had been immediate and complete. Jacob's conduct was different. Although he was born among the adherents of Yahweh, there is little sign in him, at least during the first part of his life, of the same irrepressible urge found in his grandfather, or the same trust and fervour. With Jacob, on several occasions we have been able to see hesitation born of prudence, long periods of spiritual darkness, occasionally enlightened with memories of a remote and somewhat vague God, but one who could not be completely forgotten, for this invisible protector seemed determined to keep his promises.

Thus until the incident at the ford over the Jabbok Jacob's spiritual life does not seem to offer many overt signs of progress. It was time for Yahweh to visit his chosen one again. Already at Mahanaim the encounter at the 'camp of the angels' might be considered as a serious warning. Shortly afterwards, at the night fording of the Jabbok, and despite the resistance offered to the interior voice speaking to him, Jacob must have given way. As a result, 'he supplanted' (the one who hitherto had not scrupled to lie, to deceive and even on occasion take for himself another's goods), he changed, almost at once, into 'Israel', called to become the man of God, who carried out his plans, the worthy successor of Abraham and Isaac, a firm and kindly patriarch.

That does not necessarily mean that Jacob from that day was completely transformed in his moral and social life, or that he was at once equal to the tasks awaiting him. Two trials were still necessary to complete his spiritual transformation. The first was a political matter (at Shechem); the second was the lightning-like theophany at Bethel.

The return to Shechem

Abraham, coming from Haran and for the first time entering the land of Canaan (on Yahweh's orders), made his first stop in the place that the Bible, by anticipation, calls Shechem. It was a well considered choice, for in this cool, grassy valley dominated by two well-known mountain peaks, Gerizim (2,864 feet) to the south and Ebal (3,055 feet) to the north, the shepherds could find excellent pastureland watered by the streams and springs coming from the mountains close by. With its clumps of oaks and olive trees, its rich grassland, it is a region which has delighted those who have had occasion to pass through it. At Shechem, therefore, at the Oak of Moreh, Abraham established his camp, and it was there that Yahweh appeared to him and told him, *'It is to your descendants that I will give this land'*; there too Abraham built an altar to Yahweh. We can understand how in after years Shechem came to be regarded as a holy place, before it became the first capital of the kingdom of Israel (1 Kings 12: 25).

Jacob, too, returning from Haran and making ready also to cross the land of Canaan from north to south, also settled down at Shechem. Like his grandfather he intended, it seems, to stay there for some time; he, too, built there an altar of rough stones before which he sacrificed to 'El, God of Israel'. The word used seems perhaps to indicate a stele, but whether stele or altar it will be remembered that both, regarded among the Semites as the visible dwelling of an invisible god, could receive the name of this deity (Exod. 17: 15; Judges 6: 24).

Since Abraham's time the general appearance of the countryside had perceptibly changed. In the valley Jacob could see a fortified city, recently built; this was Shechem, occupied by a tribe of Horites.[19] The prince of the country — or more accurately, perhaps, the chieftain of this foreign tribe — was called Hamor (the donkey), which was probably a totemic designation; to the city which he had just built he gave the name of his son, Shechem.

For one hundred qesitah,[20] Jacob bought the site on which his camp was established, Genesis informs us; the continuation of the narrative gives grounds for supposing that at the same time he acquired a large area of pasture-land. This was uncommon among the Semitic shepherds and still rarer among the Hebrews at the time of the patriarchs. In any case Jacob's title to this property explains the pasture rights which he was subsequently to retain over the grass lands of the Shechem valley; in addition, he probably intended to make quite sure of establishing possession over the famous Hebrew sanc-

[19] The text says Hivites or Hevites. In his translation of Genesis Fr Roland de Vaux prefers to read Horites, thus following the Greek text. The Horites, settled in this mountainous region, constituted a non-Semitic enclave. They did not therefore practise circumcision. This fact should be remembered for a proper understanding of the rest of the story.

[20] In most Bibles the reader will find 'for one hundred pieces of silver'. The Hebrew text reads *qesitah*. In any case at this period there could be no question of minted money: the silver was weighed. Coins were not to appear in Palestine until after the return from the Babylonian captivity (538 B.C.). Some versions translate *qesitah* by 'lamb'. It seems better to say that *qesitah* was a mode of exchange whose value and nature are unknown to us.

tuary which was later to be built in this place on the site where one day Joseph's tomb was to be.

Jacob may have intended to settle permanently in this verdant valley, certainly far more attractive than the scorched semi-wilderness of the Negeb, but, as we shall see, that was not Yahweh's plan for him.

At this period of his life Jacob had eleven sons. He had daughters too, but they are scarcely mentioned, though we know the name of one, Dinah, who was the heroine of a dramatic episode (Gen. 34).

One day young Shechem, Hamor's son, carried off Dinah and raped her. Shechem's act of brutality did not with Shechem rule out all trace of tenderness. For, Genesis tells us, *he was captivated* by her, *he fell in love with the young girl and comforted her.* Shechem, having made up his mind to make amends for his misdeed, asked his father to talk to the patriarch Jacob and arrange the marriage.

In the patriarchal tent a meeting took place; Jacob and his sons were present, for the latter were entitled to their say in this delicate matter in which the honour of the tribe was at stake. Some of them made no pretence of hiding their indignation. Hamor came in person to plead the cause of his heir; he even offered Jacob's people an alliance in proper form: *'Give us your daughters and take our daughters for yourselves. Stay with us and the land shall be open to you to live in or move through or own.'* Shechem asked permission to make honourable amends in the presence of the assembled family; he undertook to pay the *mohar* (dowry) at an amount to be fixed.

Then Jacob's sons, unknown to their father, plotted their revenge. Pretending to accept, at least in principle, Hamor's offer, they explained that it would however be to their dishonour to give their sisters and especially

Dinah, to uncircumcised men. As a condition for the marriage of Jacob's daughter with Hamor's son, as well as for the general alliance with the Shechemites, they insisted that the men of that tribe should be circumcised. Hamor, who for political reasons desired the fusion of the two ethnical groups, finally succeeded in obtaining the agreement of all the males of his city to this painful operation.

With adults circumcision may cause a bout of fever which is at its worst on the third day. Genesis tells us that some of the Hebrews waited until then to exact their penalty. It was not all Jacob's sons but only Simeon and Levi, Dinah's brothers (they were all three the children of Leah and so united by close ties of blood) who, taking advantage of the impaired physical condition of the Horites, marched into the fortified city of Shechem. With the help of their armed men they perpetrated a terrible massacre, putting all the men of the city (including of course Hamor and Shechem) to death by the sword. After this they ransacked the houses of the city, carried off as slaves the women and children and, in addition, seized the cattle and smaller livestock from the neighbouring farms, not forgetting the donkeys which are also mentioned in the list in Genesis. It was indeed a most successful raid.

After such a victory we might logically expect Jacob's tribe to settle down triumphantly in their newly acquired territory and establish themselves there permanently. Nothing of the sort occurred. Jacob lost no time in reprimanding those responsible for this act of war. He said to Simeon and Levi, *'You have done me harm, putting me in bad odour with the people of this land, the Canaanites and the Perizzites. I have few men, whereas they will unite against me to defeat me and destroy me and my family.'*

Jacob, as we know, was not a warlike man. Nor were his father and grandfather. One day, it is true, Abraham fell on the rear of the plundering kings who had taken Lot prisoner, but that was a case of legitimate defence for the purpose of freeing his nephew. It was an exceptional episode in the history of the Hebrew nomads. Jacob felt it better to leave this part of the country which had grown dangerous.

It is a strange story in many ways, and biblical scholars have endeavoured to explain it.

Probably two traditions – Yahwistic and Elohistic – are here combined once more and the scribe endeavoured to harmonize them as best he could.

In the first place, we have a strictly family matter. Dinah was ill-treated by Shechem; Simeon and Levi decided to avenge their sister by putting the culprit to death as well as all the members of his family, as the custom of ancient times required.

Secondly, and this is far more likely, it was a matter of rivalry between clans. Hamor, to whom the territory belonged, offered an alliance to the Hebrew clan. The sons, all the sons of Jacob, pretended to agree but they laid down as a preliminary condition the acceptance of circumcision. This enabled them to massacre the whole male population on the third day after the operation without too much risk to themselves. In the biblical account of the incident it will be noticed that Dinah appears sometimes as being with her father and sometimes with Shechem. These differences of detail in no way impair the general lines of the story.

Far more interesting is the suggestion of certain biblical scholars. In this they see the individuals named as representing clans: on one side there is Shechem, the son of Hamor, whose descendants were the Bene-

Hamor; on the other, Simeon and Levi, pastoral groups designated by the names of their heads. In short, this story amounts to an unfortunate attempt on the part of two of Jacob's companies to settle in the valley of Shechem by force. In this attempt the clans of Simeon and Levi must have played a military part. But the result was not up to their expectations. Badly knocked about and maltreated there was only one thing left for them and that was to leave the region as soon as possible.

Rather than record this defeat in the annals of the people of Israel, it was obviously better to relate it as if there had been a successful outcome. Moreover, in their archives or on their monuments, the great empires of Egypt or Syria had for long past adopted the habit of recording their most decisive defeats as glorious victories. So there was authoritative precedent for the practice. Whatever the real reason, it was urgently necessary to leave the beautiful green valley of Shechem as soon as possible; they certainly did so and not without regret.

A curious ceremony before the departure from Shechem

Yahweh remained the head of the caravan. *'Move on now,'* he commanded Jacob, *'and go to Bethel and settle there.*[21] *Make an altar there for the God who appeared to you when you were fleeing from your brother Esau.'* But before leaving, for the time being at least, for they hoped to return to this land made holy by the passage there of the great patriarch Abraham, Jacob made arrangements for a ceremony, strange yet pregnant with meaning, which offers us a curious insight into the religious reform effected in this small group whose

---

[21] This meant a fairly long stay, but not a permanent one. The objective remained Hebron where the patriarch Isaac 'full of years' was shortly to die.

chieftain, alone up to the present, adhered to the idea of the one God.

Speaking threateningly to his sons and wives, his concubines, his slaves and shepherds Jacob commanded, *'Get rid of the foreign gods you have with you; wash, and change your clothes.' They gave Jacob all the foreign gods in their possession, and the earrings that they were wearing. Jacob buried them under the oak tree near Shechem* (Gen. 35: 2–4).

'Get rid of the foreign gods you have with you,' Jacob had ordered. All these shepherds, natives of the country on the banks of the Euphrates, and the slaves carried off from the most remote regions of the Near East and the servants, were worshippers of deities originating in all sorts of different countries: Mesopotamian idols (Sumerian or Akkadian), Semitic gods (more especially those of Canaan), even those of Egypt. They formed a picturesque pantheon of wooden, copper, bronze or earthenware statues, almost always much reduced in size so that they could be easily carried about by these wandering pastoral folk continually on the move. Even Laban's daughters had kept their Aramean religion. Rachel stole her father's *teraphim* almost certainly to be able to pay homage in the privacy of her tent to the deities of her ancestors.

By his violent and general rejection of these idols Jacob firmly intended to proclaim the faith of all his people before the one God, the protector of his clan; this 'jealous' God who had no intention of sharing his glory and his worship with 'foreign gods'.

'Wash and change your clothes.' Bethel was a holy place. Now the Hebrews (and well before them the primitive Semites and also the Vedic Hindus and the Peruvians of pre-Columbus days) believed that a man could not approach a place where the deity had been

94

manifested without previously being 'sanctified', that is, 'purified'. To grasp the precise meaning of these terms we can refer to the prescriptions of the old law; obviously these are later than the period with which we are concerned, but by reason of the almost unchangeable nature of the liturgical observances of those times the historian is here on fairly solid ground.

Two days before the ceremony which was to take place in a sacred place (sometimes one day was enough) the worshipper was bound to change his clothes, or at least to wash them (Exod. 19: 10; Josh. 3: 5, 7, 13), and although there was no question of taking a bath, as was done before a profane festivity, he had to be clean when he drew near to his God. All these prescriptions are derived from very strict religious regulations. For according to the general beliefs of most primitive peoples the individual's body and his clothes could attract the spiritual powers to be found scattered about his environment. And by definition these profane entities were regarded, at least in principle, as hostile to the supernatural beings to whom homage was to be paid.

In the same way, before entering a place in which a god dwelt, sandals had to be taken off (as Moses did on Sinai when Yahweh summoned him to draw near, and the Muslims still do nowadays before entering a mosque). The same precaution was at work here: one had to avoid bringing in foreign influences on one's footwear, especially those which might come from a rival form of worship.

They gave Jacob all the foreign gods in their possession, and the earrings that they were wearing. Jacob buried them under the oak tree near Shechem (Gen. 35: 4). This was the Oak of Moreh under which Abraham had previously set up his tent. It was a venerable, historic, sacred tree in the eyes of the Hebrews.

But what was the reason for this strange burying of

the little idols, amulets and talismans? They were the *foreign gods* the Bible explains, though it seems careful not to say that they were false gods. At the time of the patriarchs neither their existence nor their power was denied. Jacob confined himself to laying down that they were undesirable.

It was only later, as the result of a spiritual evolution in accordance with the progressive character of the religion of the Chosen People, that idols were regarded by them as objects devoid of supernatural reality. The terms used to describe them in Deuteronomy (32: 21) give us an idea of the spiritual value then attributed to them: they are 'beings of nothing', 'vanity' and 'untruths'. Thus, what in Jacob's time were 'foreign gods' were to become at the time of Moses 'false gods'.

On this score there could be no question of Jacob's destroying these 'gods' by breaking them up or burning them; and it would have been impossible, or at least very dangerous, to re-use the metal after melting them down. How then could precautions be taken against the anticipated reaction of these occult powers? The best thing was to bury them deeply in the ground.

After this delicate but necessary operation Jacob's clan was now set among the followers of Yahweh, the one God.

Sojourn at Bethel

Before setting out for the holy place of Bethel Jacob informed the members of his family and his shepherds of the religious programme that he meant to carry out. *'We must move on,'* he said, *'and go to Bethel. There I will make an altar for the God who heard me when I was in distress, and gave me his help on the journey I made.'* On the uncultivated land near the village of Luz Jacob put up an altar in honour of Yahweh, a massive altar built of stones untouched by a chisel. He made a sacrifice there and prayed and gave thanks.

Yahweh did not delay in answering him. During an appearance there he confirmed the name of Israel. In addition he repeated solemnly the terms of the Covenant established with Jacob's grandfather and father, and promised him that *a group of nations shall descend from you. Even kings shall be numbered among your descendants*. And once more he stated that this land of Canaan would one day belong to the patriarch's descendants.

Jacob raised a monument in the place where he [God] *had spoken with him, a stone monument, on which he made a libation, and poured oil*. This was essentially a Semitic and typically Canaanite rite, allowed among Yahweh's followers during the period of the patriarchs but later severely condemned by the Mosaic law and by the thundering voices of the prophets (Exod. 23: 24; Lev. 26: 1; Deut. 7: 7; Hosea 3: 4; Micah 5: 12). A parallel text informs us that Jacob *named the place Bethel where God had spoken with him*. Jacob, it will be remembered, had already given the place this name on the occasion of his first halt there.

An unexpected event occurs in the middle of this chapter; this was the death of Deborah, who was buried *below Bethel, under the oak tree*. When Rebekah and her servants left Haran to come to her future husband Isaac, her nurse (mentioned but not given a name at that time) had followed her to the Negeb. How then could she now be at Bethel among Jacob's people, returning from the Land of the Fathers? Fairly obviously, this is a clumsy addition to the primitive text, wrongly incorporated in this place because of the mention of Bethel.

From Bethel to Bethel

The importance of Bethel in Jacob's life can hardly be

exaggerated. *Beth 'El,* the house of God, provides us with the key to Jacob's spiritual transformation. On his first halt at Luz (as the place was called before Jacob renamed it) he was an astute and crafty shepherd, though not without a certain maturity of mind. As was pointed out at the time, his whole wealth consisted in his shepherd's crook, but he does seem to have made up his mind not to miss an opportunity to improve matters.

To Yahweh's approaches he made a ritual response: he set up a stone on which he poured oil. He was still imbued with pagan ideas: he was afraid, indeed he was terrified (*'How awe-inspiring this place is!'*). But his heart was entirely untouched, for he at once began to lay down the conditions governing the relationship between the polytheist that he was and one of his gods. *'If God goes with me and keeps me safe on this journey I am making, if he gives me bread to eat and clothes to wear, and if I return home safe to my father, then Yahweh shall be my god. This stone I have set up as a monument shall be a house of God, and I will surely pay you a tenth part of all you have given me'* (Gen. 28: 20–22).

On his return from Haran he came to Bethel again. But this time he was at the head of a rich clan and the owner of large flocks and herds of sheep and goats, asses, cows and even camels. He had two wives, two concubines and eleven sons. Obviously, he was in a very different position from the poor shepherd of the first halt at Bethel. But there was no question now of Jacob's squaring the account in accordance with his previous undertaking, of his paying his debt to God by putting up another stele and the payment of a small levy. At that time Yahweh was not to be satisfied with a tenth of the flock; he had taken the whole man for himself. At the second visit to Bethel, and the second time of his passing through this land which had already been sanctified by Abraham's two

visits, Jacob, shortly after the astounding spiritual experience of Mahanaim, the Jabbok and Peniel, was a new man. He was entirely transformed, to put it in modern terms, by his free adhesion to the law of God or, more clearly, by his faith. It was a living, fruitful faith, ready to show itself on all occasions, and always in accordance with God's plan. After these events Jacob did not linger at Bethel; he set out for Hebron where under the oak at Mamre stood the tents of the aged patriarch Isaac. *Beth – house*
el – God

On the way from Bethel to Hebron

On the journey, at some distance from Ephrath, Rachel gave birth to a second child. It was a difficult birth in which she lost her life. *'You have another son here,'* the midwife told her joyfully. Before breathing her last Rachel wished, according to Semitic custom, to give the new-born child a name: she called him Ben-oni, that is, 'son of my sorrow'. After his wife's death Jacob decided to change this rather ominous name; the child was henceforth called Benjamin, 'son of the right hand' or 'son of happy omen'[22] which was obviously a better portent. Rachel was buried on the road to Ephrath.[23] Over her tomb Jacob raised a monument.

---

[22] The primitive meaning was 'son of the south'. Since the nomads turned to the east to take their bearings on the plains, they had the south on their right. And the south is sunlight, joy.

[23] The text of Genesis gives the geographical detail: *the road to Ephrath, at Bethlehem*. Actually, about seven-and-a-half miles from Bethlehem, near an Arab cemetery, there stands today a small Moslem sanctuary in which, according to ancient tradition, is the tomb of Rachel. Its location at this place is founded on the text quoted above (Gen. 35: 19) which biblical scholars consider to be a gloss. But there was another Ephrath, in the territory which later became that of the tribe of Benjamin: the village has disappeared, and its exact situation has been lost. Probably it should be located at Ramah if we are to believe Jeremiah (31: 15):

A voice is heard in Ramah,
lamenting and weeping bitterly;
it is Rachel weeping for her children
because they are no more.

Moreover Bethlehem (the house of bread, *Beth-lehem*) only took the name of Ephrath much later, after its occupation by a group of Ephrathites.

Jacob returns to his father's camp

Between Shechem and Hebron during the interminable journeys from pasture to pasture, Jacob must have passed through the greater part of Canaan. It might be expected that we should find in the Bible on this occasion some characteristic details concerning the moral and spiritual attitudes of Jacob in his new role. It is true of course that a little later we are shown how deep and lasting was the spiritual transformation of Yahweh's chosen one, but for the present the sacred writer seems far less interested in the study of the psychological and religious aspect than in giving the patriarch's genealogy. No doubt the scribe thought it preferable to set before us in his chronicle the names of the twelve sons of Jacob destined to become chieftains and give their names to the twelve tribes of Israel, as was fitting (see table, page 46).

What the gathering of the 'brothers' in the story of Dinah must have looked like.

Jacob the Father of the Chosen People

During the first patriarchal generation when the camp was at Bethel, Yahweh had solemnly announced to Abraham (at that time childless, and Sarah appeared to be barren): *'I will make your descendants like the dust on the ground: when men succeed in counting the grains of dust on the ground, then they will be able to count your descendants!'* Contrary to every expectation Sarah subsequently gave birth. Thus Abraham had a son, an only son, Isaac. The divine prediction had begun to be fulfilled, but in a very modest way.

In the second generation Rebekah bore Isaac the twins Esau and Jacob. But this did not amount to a number of any consequence, especially for an oriental family where the wife is usually prolific.

In the third generation with Jacob and his twelve[24] sons, matters improve and we can begin to see the possibility of a rapid increase of the family. It was in fact through Jacob-Israel that the little Hebrew clan became a confederation of tribes.

Clan and tribe, two terms that require explanation. The nomad had no idea at all of what is meant by a State. The basis of the social organization of these wandering shepherds was of course the family. If the head of the family possessed a certain affluence he would have a number of servants and slaves and, if he had several flocks to be watched over at pasture he would engage shepherds. Thus would be formed the clan, typical instances of which we have already encountered in those of Abraham and Lot, the clan which Isaac inherited from

[24] Twelve: this number of fullness in connection with descendants (as was mentioned above) is found elsewhere. Ishmael (the son of Abraham and the Egyptian concubine Hagar) also had twelve sons who became chiefs of the twelve tribes of Ishmaelites. And Esau, too, had twelve sons who became chiefs of the twelve tribes of Edomites. And we know, too, that Nahor, Abraham's brother, also had twelve sons. It can probably be conjectured that this number is conventional in view of its well-known symbolism.

his father, and that formed by Jacob in the land of the Euphrates.

If the father of the family, the chieftain of the clan (or patriarch) had many sons and if, in addition, he came to be the owner of a large amount of livestock, it would be necessary to divide the flocks, either when the inheritance was shared out or even, on occasion, beforehand. Each son would then leave with his share of the livestock in search of grass and water in an attempt to make his property bear fruit. In this way new clans were formed which remained, of course, closely linked with the original group in brotherly fellowship and still more by religious ties. Together all these clans scattered over the region, but closely united by the same family spirit and ancestral religion, formed the tribe.

The appearance in the Bible story of Jacob's twelve sons foreshadows the impending splitting up of the primitive clan. One day Jacob, who was already the owner of large flocks, would inherit his father's property; this would be bound to raise serious problems regarding pasture and it would become necessary as a result to send out the shepherds with their flocks to considerable distances from each other. The examples of Abraham and Lot form an illustration of the practical application of this law. Henceforward each son would be called on to form a clan which, in the normal course, would give rise to a new tribe. Twelve sons: twelve tribes. This was the perfectly normal social evolution in the patriarchal organization of these shepherds.

When did the twelve tribes appear in history? They were not in existence during the lifetime of Jacob, for all his sons were still employed in looking after the sheep as shepherds for their father. Thus during the nomadic period there were no separate Hebrew tribes. In the strict sense of the word, during the time of the patriarchs, the term clan can only be used for those of Abraham, Isaac and Jacob and, at one moment, for that of Esau. Nor were the twelve tribes formed at the time of Jacob's death. When this occurred the clan was in Egypt, summoned by Joseph (Jacob's son) who had established himself there with considerable financial and political success. The same can be said when Joseph died, for after his death there was a further change in the attitude of the Egyptian government; the Hebrew clan, settled in the Delta, found itself reduced to the wretched position of slaves, forced to perform the hard, exhausting and inhuman work of carrying bricks for the construction of the colossal buildings put up by the pharaohs of the nineteenth dynasty.

The first clear mention of the twelve tribes occurs a good five hundred years after Jacob[25] when on Sinai Moses ratified the Covenant of the Chosen People with Yahweh (Exod. 24: 3 following). There is a more precise mention of the twelve tribes at the renewal of the Covenant in the famous valley of Shechem (Jos. 24). It is only in these circumstances that we can see the federal structure of the twelve tribes who regarded themselves as the political posterity of Jacob-Israel.

The figure of twelve tribes is traditional, but it has varied down the ages. Nevertheless we can now see why the scribe thought it necessary to recall here the names of the twelve sons of Israel.

Death and burial of Isaac

A very short paragraph is devoted to these events. *Jacob reached the house of his father Isaac at . . . Hebron . . .*

[25] The approximate dates are, Jacob, *c.* 1800–1750 B.C.; Moses and Joshua, 1200 B.C.

Isaac . . . died and was gathered to his people. . . . His sons Esau and Jacob buried him. There is not a word to tell what welcome was given to Jacob on his return after so long an absence, there is nothing about Rebekah, and there is nothing about the burial which took place in the nearby cave of Machpelah where the bodies of Abraham and his wife Sarah already lay. Esau and Jacob, the two brothers once more together, performed their filial duty at their father's grave. The account could not be more laconic.

Who was Isaac's heir?

In accordance with the law prevailing at the time Esau was regarded as the elder. There had of course occurred the abandonment of the birthright in exchange for the plate of soup, but that question remained to some extent open. More complicated was the theft of Isaac's blessing, for such a blessing was irreversible and could not be annulled. As will be remembered it had invested Jacob as chief of the clan. The question arose acutely whether in the last resort Esau would allow himself to be ousted by Jacob (*he has supplanted*).

The writer glosses over these family matters. Yet it is notorious, even in modern Europe, how the division of an inheritance raises difficulties and often leads to heated argument and lawsuits. And it may be guessed what a similar situation could provoke in the ancient East. But contrary to expectation we find Esau putting his baggage together[26] and setting out for the land of Edom. *Esau, taking his wives, his sons and daughters, all the members*

---

[26] The Priestly tradition (P) which probably furnished the materials for the scribe in writing this passage shows us Esau as living up to this time with his father Isaac at Hebron. But as we have seen above (p. 86) the Yahwistic (J) and Elohistic (E) cycles suppose that long before Isaac's death Esau had settled far from his father in the land of Edom, though it is very difficult to see how this could be.

of his household, his livestock, all his cattle and all the goods he had acquired in the land of Canaan, left for the land of Seir [Edom] *away from his brother Jacob. For they had acquired too much to live together. The land in which they were at that time could not support them both because of their livestock* (Gen. 36: 6–7). The author of the biblical text makes a point of showing the separation of the two brothers, formerly at enmity but now reconciled, arising naturally from the amount of livestock. And it is certainly surprising to find the quick-tempered, brutish Esau, who in the past had desired to kill his brother because he had stolen his birthright, agree to his own elimination in a spirit of complete and utter renunciation. Without protest Esau, much milder it is true since the encounter with Jacob shortly after the fording of the Jabbok, allowed his younger brother to take over their father's pasturelands and position as chieftain. All ended for the best, the scribe assures us.

But he writes at much greater length when it is a matter of giving the list of the kings of Edom and the genealogy of the descendants of Esau; practically a whole chapter of Genesis (36) is devoted to the subject. It must be admitted that it holds little interest for the modern reader, especially as here again several traditions are drawn upon and the various explanations do not always agree; the scribe himself is sometimes confused. We can leave the orientalist to consider why the title of the kings of Edom is of Horite origin and also why the names of some of the wives are changed on occasion into the names of chieftains. Nevertheless, the long recitation of complicated genealogies was very popular in the East and the story-tellers liked to indulge their audiences.

The conclusion of the story of Jacob

Esau left the patriarchal camp of Hebron and we hear no more about him. The history of Israel continues with Jacob.

Jacob had pitched camp a short distance from the little city of Hebron, at the Oak of Mamre, a spot favoured by the patriarchs ever since Abraham was first there. Logically, we might expect to find Jacob settling down as a shrewd administrator of his property, a careful sheep-farmer who continued to remain faithful to Yahweh. After which it would be quite normal to see the old patriarch 'full of years' and surrounded by his sons reach the end of his earthly existence in the same peaceful way as his grandfather and father.

Events did not turn out like that. Jacob can hardly have imagined that he would have to go on another long journey to a foreign land. Nor could he have expected that once more he would have to undergo severe moral trials. Certainly he could not have foreseen that later on he would have to leave the Promised Land to die on the banks of the Nile.

Nevertheless, after Jacob had settled at Hebron the Bible informs us that this is the end of the history of Jacob. Not that he disappears completely from the scene. We shall subsequently find him playing a certain part, but a very secondary one, it must be admitted. For very shortly the important person in whom all the interest of the story lies is Joseph, Jacob's favourite son. And it is this which concerns us in the next chapter.

3

JOSEPH: THE EGYPTIAN ADVENTURE

The story of Joseph's adventures forms a sharp contrast with the preceding chapters. From the point of view of literary style, in the first place, there is a portrayal of character which is novel and rather romantic in its general effect. A sequence of events is set off against a background that is sometimes dramatic; in addition the observation of detail has often provoked the admiration of the Egyptologists – the most important part of Joseph's life was spent in Egypt. The careful construction of the work is also worthy of notice. The lives of Abraham, Isaac and Jacob were put before us in a series of pictures, colourful, no doubt, but often placed side by side without obvious connection; the story of Joseph, on the other hand, unfolds before us in logical order, one event leading to another and all set down in a vigorous style.

The literary side is important, but it must not be forgotten that the Bible is principally the history of the revelation of the one God to his People. And here we notice an appreciable change in the relationship between Yahweh and his creature. In the life of Joseph, and unlike what we have so far encountered, there is no more direct, peremptory and almost, it might seem, visible action on the part of Yahweh. With Joseph Yahweh does not disappear from the scene in the story, and he certainly continues to guide his chosen ones, always in pursuance of the realization of his plan. The Promise, the Covenant, was still in force. But in Egypt Yahweh seems to act in that secret, unforeseen and fruitful way known to Christians as Providence. Thus the criminal plot hatched by Joseph's brothers was unexpectedly transformed into a blessing firstly for Joseph himself, then for the clan and even for those who had plotted to murder him. The conspiracy set on foot by Joseph's brothers resulted not in his moral rebellion, nor in the destruction of his legitimate hopes, but in his spiritual progress, social success and the happiness of his family. In addition, there was the pardon of the guilty parties. All this stamps the story with a lofty moral tone considerably in advance of its period, and accounts probably for its popularity in successive generations.

Despite the apparent simplicity of the material for this chapter it requires, I believe, a certain amount of explanation, especially for that part of it relating to Egypt. From time to time, also, historical commentaries on certain points will prove valuable. This is the more necessary since certain Egyptologists have in recent years made a critical examination of Joseph's adventures;[1] and there are certain odd coincidences requiring emphasis which on many points show the authenticity of the biblical narrative.

Joseph's life-story can be divided up as follows:
Early life at Hebron.
Joseph sold by his brothers.

---

[1] I must mention here particularly the book by J. Vergotte, *Joseph en Egypte*, Publications Universitaires de Louvain, 1959. He is an Egyptologist who has made a critical appraisal of the linguistic, historical and archaeological problems that are raised by the subject of Joseph after his transplantation to Egypt. In this chapter I have adopted some of the conclusions of this eminent Egyptologist.

The unexpected encounter in Egypt between Joseph and
his brothers.

The end of the Egyptian adventure.

In conclusion, there is a short epilogue which enables us
to see the natural connection with the following period,
a very different one in all respects both in its dramatic
content and religious spirit. We shall be dealing with the
period in which arose the brilliant personality of Moses,
the prophet, lawgiver and leader of the people of God.

Early life at Hebron

The scene is set in the valley of Hebron, among the tents
of Jacob-Israel. The Hebrew chieftain, the possessor of
large flocks, had ten grown-up sons to whom he could
entrust the supervision and leading of his flocks from
pasture to pasture, often in very remote regions. Jacob
himself scarcely moved from the old camp in which
Abraham and Isaac had previously settled and died. It
was a quiet life, at least as a rule. But the malice of men,
and of women, was to be reckoned with: there were deep
resentments, and a smouldering hostility which quickly
reached the point of exasperation in this life of a closed
community. Little was needed to arouse resentment, and
to engender implacable hatreds.

Joseph, Jacob's favourite son

Joseph was now sixteen. He was a fine youth, intelligent,
and of a frank and open character. Like his younger
brother Benjamin, he was the son of Rachel, Jacob's
wife who had died on the way to Ephrath. Soon Jacob's
preference for Joseph became obvious and naturally it
provoked a latent jealousy among the ten elder brothers.
A further complication was caused by Joseph's pro-
pensity for reporting to his father the criticisms of which
the latter was the object. For to teach him his trade

Joseph was sent out to shepherd the flocks with his half-brothers, the sons of the concubines Bilhah and Zilpah; this provided an excellent opportunity for him to hear any slanderous gossip in circulation, all of which he repeated to Jacob. The other brothers were considerably displeased at this behaviour and began to join forces against Joseph.

At this juncture Jacob committed a blunder; he gave orders for a fine *coat with long sleeves* to be made for Joseph. It was one of those handsome embroidered full-length garments which were in vogue for women and even youths of good family. Thereupon his brothers *came to hate him so much that they could not say a civil word to him*. Hostilities were declared.

The Bible and dreams

We come now to Joseph's two ominous dreams which he was to tell, rather rashly, to his father and brothers. Before we consider this part of the story it will be useful to examine the attitude of the Old Testament to dreams and their interpretation.

We have already encountered dreams which played a certain part in the stories in Genesis — the dreams of Abraham in which Yahweh entrusted him with definite missions; Abimelech's dream in which Yahweh told him to return Sarah to her husband; Jacob's dream at the time of his first halt at Bethel. Subsequently, throughout the history of Israel, we shall discover many other examples of these nocturnal visitations. Does this mean that according to the Bible a dream is to be regarded as a real, authentic premonition, a warning from God who thus shows us his will? Is it true that God is willing thus to show us the future?

The whole of oriental antiquity in the first place, and

110

subsequently Greek and Roman civilization, attached the greatest importance to dreams. At this period of his life Joseph was at Hebron, in a social environment still permeated with Mesopotamian memories and customs brought from Ur and also from Haran by Abraham's clan. Now according to the Babylonian view dreams possessed a reality of their own. It mattered little that they occurred during sleep; the warning remained just as valid as if it had taken place in a waking state. Indeed it was believed that the individual when asleep was in a more receptive condition and that it was easier for him to enter into relations with the deity. Obviously when the theme of the dream was incoherent and really strange it required explanation. The Mesopotamians, like the Egyptians, sought out soothsayers who were specialists in this branch. The inhabitants of Canaan, under the influence of Egypt and Mesopotamia, were almost bound to adopt these same religious ideas.

In this case the position of the Bible seems to vary. We find, of course, the sacred writer telling us with all the assurance of a modern historian the revelations received in their sleep by certain chosen persons who might have been favoured with a vision (an interior one in most cases) during the day. But in addition to these exceptional nocturnal communications, which the Bible records with particular care, it makes a point also of putting us on our guard against seeking a systematic explanation of our ordinary dreams. Unlike the two great civilizations surrounding it, the small Hebrew clan, which was later to become the People of Israel, believed that it was wholly futile, even dangerous, to endeavour to discover the meaning of our dreams. The following passage from Ecclesiasticus, despite its relatively late date (second century B.C.) gives us a general idea of the attitude of the more advanced Hebrews on this problem:

Dreams put fools in a flutter.
As well clutch at shadows and chase the wind
as put any faith in dreams.
Mirror and dream are similar things:
confronting a face, the reflection of that face.
What can be cleansed by uncleanness,
what can be verified by falsehood?
Divinations, auguries and dreams are nonsense,
like delirious fancies of a pregnant woman.
Unless sent as emissaries from the Most High,
do not give them a thought;
for dreams have led many astray,
and those building their hopes on them have been
disappointed.

(Sirach 34: 1–7)

In the same way we shall find lawgivers and prophets strictly forbidding recourse to dreams to discover the future or furnish guidance in daily life. It is no less true that in certain very special cases the Bible admits that God may manifest himself in a dream; inherent in such a direct revelation is so great a spiritual power that a creature favoured by them would find it impossible to doubt their transcendent nature. Thus while Ben Sirach, the author of Ecclesiasticus, bids us give no credit to our dreams, he is careful to add *Unless sent as emissaries from the Most High*.

Thus the faithful follower of Yahweh was required to exercise scrupulous discrimination in the matter. Joseph's dreams, it cannot be doubted, were divine premonitions irrupting into a human condition in which the providence of Yahweh, the protector of the Hebrew clan, was soon to show itself with startling results.

112

Joseph's two premonitory dreams

Joseph's first dream, which unfortunately for him he hastened to tell his brothers, depicted all Jacob's sons in a field busy at the harvest; the time had come to bind the sheaves. Suddenly Joseph's sheaf stood upright while all the others gathered round and bowed to his sheaf. This was a prefiguring of the scene, which actually happened, when Joseph's brothers, to combat the terrible famine then raging in Canaan, came to the Egyptian territory of the Delta to ask for help. Without recognizing the man who fifteen years previously they had sold for a slave, they bowed low, their heads in the dust, before Joseph, who at that time, had unexpectedly become viceroy of Egypt.

Those times had not yet come. But Joseph's brothers, in true eastern fashion, detected some sort of symbolic lesson. *'So you want to be king over us,'* they retorted, *'or to lord it over us?'* And Genesis adds: *And they hated him still more, on account of his dreams and of what he said*.

The second dream was as strange as the first. Joseph told this one also to his family, *'I thought I saw the sun,'* he said, *'the moon and eleven stars, bowing to me.'* The sun obviously referred to Jacob, his father, the moon to Rachel, his mother, [2] and the eleven stars to his eleven brothers. This time Joseph was sharply reproved by Jacob – he had no desire for this adolescent to imagine that all his family would one day bow down before him.

Jacob had lived in Upper Mesopotamia for too long to remain indifferent to these premonitory dreams. Despite the scolding he gave to his favourite son he foresaw for him an unusual destiny. *His father kept the*

---

[2] It will probably be objected that at this time Rachel was no longer alive. It is likely that this version belongs to a cycle which places Rachel's death at a later period.

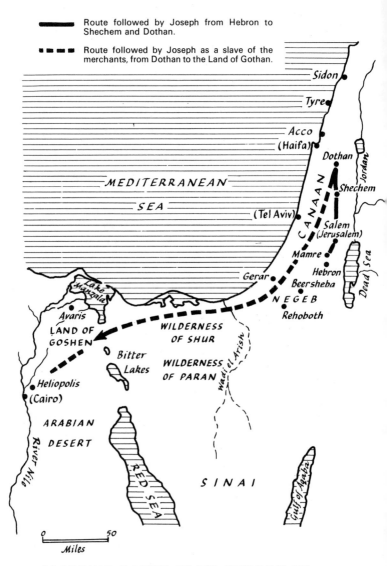

Legend:

──────── Route followed by Joseph from Hebron to Shechem and Dothan.

▬ ▬ ▬ ▬ Route followed by Joseph as a slave of the merchants, from Dothan to the Land of Gothan.

Sidon

Tyre

Acco (Haifa)

Dothan

Shechem

Jordan

MEDITERRANEAN

SEA

(Tel Aviv)

CANAAN

Salem (Jerusalem)

Mamre

Gerar

Hebron
Beersheba

Dead Sea

NEGEB

Rehoboth

Lake Manzala

Avaris

LAND OF GOSHEN

WILDERNESS OF SHUR

WILDERNESS OF PARAN

Wadi el Arish

Bitter Lakes

Heliopolis (Cairo)

ARABIAN DESERT

River Nile

RED SEA

SINAI

Gulf of Aqaba

0   50
Miles

JOSEPH'S ROUTE FROM HEBRON TO DOTHAN, DOTHAN TO EGYPT

thing in mind, [3] says Genesis; he awaited the future with confidence.

The ten brothers, on the other hand, were out of all patience with these disquieting prophetic dreams.

The Plot

Jacob, who remained at his headquarters at Hebron, sent the greater part of his smaller livestock (sheep and goats) to the pastures of Shechem; it seems certain, therefore, that for his fifty *qesitah* the patriarch had acquired unquestionable rights of pasture in this region. Of course, another portion of his flocks continued to graze neighbouring plains of the Negeb. Under the supervision of the ten brothers a considerable number of sheep and goats had been moved to the valley of Shechem. A patriarch as careful of his interests as Jacob likes to be informed regularly of the state of his flocks; for this purpose he decided to send his young son Joseph to Shechem for news.

On arrival at the place where he could have expected to find his brothers Joseph could see no one. A man belonging to the neighbourhood told him where they were: *'Your brothers have moved on from here; indeed I heard them say, "Let us go to Dothan"'.* Dothan is a small place situated some twenty miles to the north, now known as Tel Dotan. The present village stands on an artificial hillock formed by the debris of the various buildings which down the centuries have fallen into ruin on top of each other. From a height of nearly a hundred feet it dominates a plain (Sahel 'Arrabeh) watered by springs and a wandering stream. The countryside has retained its pleasant character: there are orchards of oranges and

---

[3] An expression which may be compared with those used by St Luke in speaking of the Blessed Virgin: firstly, at the birth of Jesus and then during his hidden life at Nazareth: *As for Mary she treasured all these things and pondered them in her heart* (Luke 2: 19). *His mother stored up all these things in her heart* (Luke 2: 51).

Time for sheep-shearing. A lot of work, but afterwards tremendous public rejoicing.

lemons, fig trees, grassland. In many places there are water tanks hewn out of the limestone. We can be fairly certain that it was in this pastoral setting that Jacob's sons had set up their tents when Joseph came to find them.

From a distance they saw their young brother, who was easy to recognize because of his long coat. *'Here comes the man of dreams,'* they said one to another. *'Come on, let us kill him,'* one of them suggested. *'We can say that a wild beast devoured him,'* added a third, *'then we shall see what becomes of his dreams.'* Reuben, the eldest, intervened. His behaviour towards his father had not always been blameless and possibly he had no desire to have another crime on his conscience. *'We must not take his life,'* he said. *'Shed no blood, throw him into this well in the wilderness, but do not lay violent hands on him.'* Reuben hoped to save Joseph's life and return him one day safe and sound to his father. A few lines further on (Gen. 37: 26) we are told that it was Judah who was responsible for the measures to save Joseph's life. [4]

The water tanks were hewn out of the rock and in the rainy season were filled by various methods from the water in the neighbourhood. Thus in a watertight tank

The Priestly code (P) whose documentary materials are used here from time to notice numerous and perceptible inconsistencies in the narrative. This is explained by the fact that the scribe who, in about the sixth century B.C., wrote down the text of the Pentateuch which we now have, made use of various traditions (they are also termed cycles, sources or codes) which he reverently collected and faithfully recorded with the eagerness of an archivist. It should be remembered that these 'cycles' were preserved for five centuries in oral form (at the time of the nomads they were recited fervently by the story-tellers) and a beginning was made in writing them down about the time of David (about 1000 B.C.). It was the chapters of these traditions, differing on occasion in detail, which were transcribed by the scribe in the sixth century.

The following are the characteristics of the three cycles whose presence it is possible to discern in the account of the life of Joseph:

The Yahwistic cycle (or J, because God is designated by the name Yahweh). It is in a popular, brisk, narrative style.

The Elohistic cycle (or E, thus called because God is designated by the name Elohim).

the precious liquid was kept for those months when the sun dried up the springs and wells. These tanks must not be confused with the bathing-pools, also common in Canaan, which were open to the sky. The usual form of water tank was bottle shaped. There was a small narrow opening, like the neck of a bottle (to lessen the risk of pollution) giving access to a chamber, round or square, generally of medium size, but the side could be as much as one hundred feet long. The opening was carefully closed with a stone (like the wells in the wilderness) or with logs of wood. In these tanks water kept very fresh and was safe from evaporation. The wandering shepherds often took care to flatten the ground all round the openings so that they alone could recognize the presence of this underground reservoir on which, at least at certain times of the year, depended the lives of their flocks.

Frequently in the history of Israel we find abandoned water tanks used as places of refuge, especially at the time of the Philistine invasions. Sometimes they were transformed into prisons (Jer. 36: 6–13). Into one of these dismal and dark places (the precaution was certainly taken of stopping up the opening) the unfortunate Joseph was unceremoniously thrown.

The Priestly code (P) whose documentary materials are used here from time to time in the enumeration of the genealogies. God is called by the name El Shaddai (the Rock?).

The sixth-century scribe respected his texts to a great degree, and endeavoured to collect together as much as possible of the ancient cycles; he partially recopied them, placing them side by side even if they recorded the same events in different ways. Thus in the dramatic anecdote which has just been related, which comes from the E cycle, it is Reuben who prevents the brothers from killing Joseph, and the latter is to be sold shortly afterwards to a caravan of Midianite merchants; whereas in the J cycle he proposes instead to sell Joseph to a caravan of Ishmaelites.

These differences of detail will not surprise the reader if he knows the reason for the variations. The use of these traditions endows the Pentateuch with an indisputable stamp of authenticity. It can be seen that the author of the final draft took every possible precaution to go back to the most authoritative source material, and we cannot blame him for not having made use of the latest methods of work of historical science. It remains true nonetheless that his blunders constitute an undeniable proof of his honesty as an historian.

Joseph: The Egyptian Adventure

Joseph sold by his brothers

After this exploit the brothers sat down to eat. They had hardly finished their meal when they saw a group of merchants with camels on their way down to Egypt. They hailed the merchants and for twenty pieces of silver the bargain was concluded: Joseph was taken from his dark prison and the merchants led him away to be a slave in Egypt.

These merchants, we are told, were Ishmaelites (J cycle) and, a few lines farther down, Midianites (E cycle). The non-specialist reader might well think that this divergence is of little importance. It is nonetheless interesting to note that at the time of the patriarchs the export of spices, gathered and processed in the eastern countries and destined for Egypt, was almost exclusively in the hands of Ishmaelite and Midianite merchants.

The question of the camels is more difficult. Some scholars have stated that the camel was only domesticated towards the end of the twelfth century B.C., thus a good five hundred years after the time of Joseph, and they point out that Egyptian monuments show no representations of camels before this date. This theory is disproved by the recent discovery of silhouettes of camels dating from the predynastic period (before the year 3000). We know from other sources that the camel was used in Arabia in the fifth, or at least the fourth millennium, but it did not make its appearance in the Near East until a much later period. In Egypt the ground was too slippery for camels, but they were probably adopted at an early date by the patriarchs and used by them even when they were travelling with their flocks on the plains of Canaan. On his return from his journey to Egypt Abraham went back to Hebron with camels. Later on he sent his confidential slave to Haran to find a wife of Aramean blood for his son Isaac and the journey there and back was performed on the back of a camel. So there is probably no anachronism here.

Another historical detail which gives the account an undeniably authentic character is the list of the various spices carried by the caravan which, we are told, was coming from Gilead: *Their camels were laden with gum tragacanth, balsam and resin, which they were taking down into Egypt.* Gum tragacanth is a form of resinous substance gathered from the bushes of the species Astragalus; it was used by the ancients as an astringent remedy. *Sere,* the Hebrew name of the product which is translated by balsam, was gathered and prepared in the Canaanite region of Gilead. Now the passage of Genesis takes care to tell us that the merchants to whom Joseph was sold came in fact from Gilead. From other sources we know that the Egyptians were heavy buyers of this balsam which was applied to wounds.

The resin referred to flows from the trunk or even from the branches of a kind of rose-tree extensively cultivated in Canaan. The Egyptians burned this sweet-smelling substance in the temples and also in private houses. It was also used in the manufacture of certain cosmetics; it was applied to certain parts of the body to relieve pain and was also used to prevent the hair turning grey or falling out. All these typically Canaanite products, archaeology has discovered, were very popular in the Egyptian markets.

We have by no means come to an end of the historical proofs which seem to proliferate on every page and which help to authenticate the facts of the narrative. Thus we are told by the writers, whose account was based on ancient sources of dependable authenticity, that the brothers sold Joseph to the Ishmaelites who took him to Egypt. This was no chance occurrence. Asia, and more especially Canaan, was regarded by the Egyptians as the source of the best slaves; for this reason men of the regions that are now Palestine and Syria fetched the highest prices on the market. Sometimes, and already by the time of the Middle Empire (2000–1800), a Canaanite was designated in Egypt by the name of *aam*, that is, slave. The Midianites and the Ishmaelites, with their camels and spices, on occasion, therefore, in addition trafficked in slave labour. All this agrees with what Genesis has to tell us.

Cruel sequel

Not content with having sold their brother, Jacob's sons did not hesitate to cause their father the most grievous affliction. Perhaps they thought to take secret revenge for his marked preference for Joseph. They took the coat, given to Joseph by his father, and dipped it in the blood of a goat killed for the purpose. Then with feigned sorrow they brought it to their father. *'Examine it,'* they said, *'and see whether or not it is your son's coat.'* Jacob on one occasion tricked his father; in his turn he was now tricked by his own sons. When he saw the fine cloth torn and stained the old man had no difficulty in reconstructing the scene: *'A wild beast has devoured him,'* he exclaimed, *'Joseph has been the prey of some animal and has been torn to pieces!'*

There was nothing very surprising about this. It was one of the occupational hazards in the hard life of the Semitic shepherds who had to defend themselves night and day against the attacks of wild beasts which were always on the watch to fall upon a sheep which strayed even a short way from the rest of the flock. One of the most dangerous of the wild animals was the lion which could easily find a lair in the thorny thickets of the valley of the Jordan. The Old Testament mentions lions something like one hundred and thirty times, which gives us some idea of the fear they caused to the shepherds; lions disappeared from the Holy Land at the time of the crusades when they were exterminated by the knights who had come to fight the Saracens. There were also leopards, constantly on the prowl whose rapidity of movement was proverbial. Wolves, too, could sometimes prove formidable opponents and the bear, also, or rather the female bear at the time when she was suckling her young. There were many and incessant dangers facing the shepherds on the plains.

Confronted with the blood-stained coat, which told its own story, Jacob could abandon any hope of seeing his beloved son alive. He thus tore his clothes (for the purpose of making himself unrecognizable to the spirit of the dead youth, which by definition was dreaded and dangerous). Then he put on the well-known *saq* (described at length in the preceding volume devoted to Abraham, in the chapter concerning Sarah's funeral); this, it will be remembered, was a kind of loin cloth of rough material or very coarse leather which was tied round the waist.

Jacob then received the condolences of his daughters and, rather revoltingly, of his sons, the authors of the crime. But Jacob refused to be comforted: *'No,'* he said, *'I will go down in mourning to Sheol!'* What exactly did he mean by that?

At first sight it might be thought that in his affliction Jacob had decided to wear the *saq*, the garment of mourning, until his death. Something has already been said here about Sheol (see page 1), but to elucidate Jacob's remark it should be added that in the subterranean dwelling where the 'shades' of the dead were gathered, the dead person's 'double' continued to live a diminished existence, rather like the Egyptian *ka*; and in this dark and sombre place the dead person retained the appearance and even the clothes of the moment of death. For example, at the time of the Kings, when the ghost of Samuel was conjured up by a necromancer, the old 'judge of Israel' was wrapped in the cloak which he had been wearing at the time of his death (1 Sam. 28: 14). In Sheol monarchs retained the insignia of their high office, old men could be recognized by their white hair, the warrior who had died fighting still showed the marks of his wounds. Thus, in the present case, Jacob desired to lead the slower-paced life in Sheol wearing the garments symbolizing his despair. *And his father wept for him.*

Meanwhile the young man who was officially dead arrived safe and sound in Egypt with the merchants' caravan; there he was at once sold as a slave to Potiphar *one of Pharaoh's officials and commander of the guard.*

The political state of Egypt at the time of Joseph (about 1650–1600)

As a general rule the Egyptians of antiquity were opposed to foreigners. In the ports of the Delta or of the Red Sea, and at the frontier posts on land, foreign merchants bringing products or raw materials needed for Pharaoh's court, for the temples or the workshops, were readily welcomed. If in some cases it was necessary to allow foreigners to establish trading posts the Egyptian officials took care to assign them a definite city as a residence, where they were confined to special quarters from which they were forbidden to leave. Whether they were Libyans from the west, Canaanites from the east or Nubians from the south all these foreigners were invariably regarded with marked distrust by the Egyptians.

Now in the part of the story with which we are shortly to be concerned we shall discover Joseph the Hebrew quickly attaining the highest imaginable honours in

Egypt: the young shepherd, the son of Jacob, a Canaanite shepherd, was not long in becoming the *vizier*, the first minister of the powerful sovereign. He was to be invested with the highest office after that of the monarch himself, receiving the title of viceroy. Genesis gives a careful description of Joseph's investiture (Egyptologists agree as to its accuracy): Pharaoh took the ring from his own finger and put it on Joseph's as a sign of his trust in him, and placed a heavy gold chain round his neck.

This story of a Semite achieving high office at the Egyptian court appears difficult to accept: the castes were kept so entirely separate, and in high government circles there was a very marked antipathy for everything foreign. Asiatics, Canaanites particularly, were heartily disliked and no secret was made of it. In these circumstances Joseph's extraordinary Egyptian adventure as told in Genesis, the rapid rise of an unimportant Hebrew to a high position in Pharaoh's court, might well, it seems, have been invented for reasons of prestige. And on this score an argument has been advanced against the authenticity of the story.

As it happens history sheds a certain light on this chapter of Genesis. In Joseph's time (which can be dated approximately between 1650 and 1600 B.C.) Egypt was no longer in the hands of native rulers. Already for one hundred and fifty years, perhaps even for two centuries, lower Egypt had endured the harsh occupation of peoples of largely Asiatic origin, called by the Egyptians the Hyksos (or shepherd kings, but this translation is uncertain). In these circumstances it is historically if not geographically inaccurate to say simply that Joseph was extraordinarily successful 'in Egypt'. For although he did build up a large fortune in the land of Egypt that country was then occupied, militarily and socially, by Asiatic invaders, who at that time were masters of the country and its destiny. Knowledge of this fact helps us to understand better how with the help of these Asiatics and for their own benefit, Joseph, racially closely related to them, managed to attain almost to royal status.

Thus Joseph's adventure is seen to be wholly acceptable, indeed it fits in neatly with the historical context; we have an occupying power when the opportunity occurs making use in its administrative plans of a man of its own country of origin.

There is no need here to go back over the long and turbulent history of the Hyksos which in many ways, indeed, is rather obscure. But since Joseph's rise to power occurred within the framework of the Hyksos occupation of Egypt and can only be explained by it the following rapid historical summary will help to make matters clear.

At the beginning of the eighteenth century B.C. the Hyksos invaded the Near East in formidable waves, suddenly appearing from various regions of Asia. It is probable that this human tide was set in motion under the pressure of Indo-Aryan tribes which attacked Media. This was the cause of great upheaval among all the peoples who were more or less settled in the north and the north-east of Mesopotamia. Events were complicated by the fact that, as these hordes advanced, some of the ethnical groups unsettled by all this disturbance joined the invaders, who after overrunning Mesopotamia advanced on Canaan and fell like a swarm of locusts on the rich land of Egypt.

The victory of the invading hordes can be explained by their use of new arms against which the Egyptian soldiers had no defense. These warriors from remote parts of Asia used chariots drawn by horses, an animal at that time unknown in the Near East. We may well

imagine the surprise and the terror caused by the appearance on a battle field of this weapon which broke through
the infantry lines, opened breaches in the marching
columns and fell unexpectedly on the rear of the enemy.
In addition the Hyksos possessed considerable superiority
in arms over the Egyptians. The latter began their attacks
with a primitive form of bow provided with arrows made
of ebony-tipped reeds; for hand to hand fighting they
used copper battle-axes, clubs and daggers; even at the

**Armour consists of metal plates sewn onto a garment made of
skin.**

time of the Middle Empire (2000–1800 B.C.) they were
still at the stage of wooden swords which had been
hardened in the fire. The arms of the Hyksos were very
different. They used a powerful bow made of several
layers of flexible wood, strengthened with horn; their
arrow heads were metal and therefore sharp. To protect
his body the warrior wore a kind of tunic very like the
coat of mail of the medieval knights, that is, a leather
garment on which were sewn plates of copper. Lastly,

126

the Hyksos' sword was made of bronze, in the form of a two-edged scimitar which could be used with both hands at once. It is hard to see how the Egyptian army with the arms at its disposal could have withstood these well-armed hordes.

The Jewish historian Josephus (A.D. 37–92), referring to the historian Manetho (third century B.C.), quotes a few sentences from the latter (whose works have been lost) to give us an idea of the brutality of this Hyksos invasion. 'I hardly know how the wrath of God,' explains Manetho, 'was unleashed upon us, and without warning a people of unknown race, coming from the East, had the effrontery to invade our country. On account of their strength they seized it without striking a blow' [a slight exaggeration: it would be more accurate to say that they entirely overran the Egyptian defences] 'seized our leaders, burnt down the cities, razed the temples of the gods to the ground and treated the natives with the greatest cruelty, massacring some of them, and carrying off the children and women as slaves. . . .' Without necessarily taking the Hyksos' side it must be acknowledged that they followed the military law of the times, the same law applied by the Egyptians in their victorious expeditions beyond the Nile valley.

The actual result of all this was that these Indo-Aryans, surrounded by a mixture of different peoples who had followed them and served as auxiliaries, settled with evident satisfaction in Egypt. Despite their brutality as soldiers the Hyksos cannot be regarded as primitive or as barbarians, at any rate so far as the governing classes were concerned. The newcomers to Egypt possessed sufficient perception and intelligence to recognize quite clearly that the civilization with which they had so roughly come into contact was superior to their own. After their extraordinary success, therefore, they set about adopting the customs of the Egyptians, they copied their art and endeavoured to carry on their traditions so far as possible. They did their best to become Egyptians. In imitation of their predecessors several of the Hyksos sovereigns adopted the title of Pharaoh.

Huyan, one of the Hyksos princes, went on to establish a vast empire which extended to the north-east as far as the Tigris and in the south included Egypt as its boundary. Avaris his capital was established in Egypt. Archaeologists have discovered a seal bearing his name with the proud title 'Master of the country'. Thus in the northern sector of the course of the Nile the Hyksos were established, taking the place of the national dynasty which they had just overthrown, adopting the religion and customs of the invaded country and soon passing themselves off as real Egyptians.

Such were the conditions in the country when Joseph arrived there, and was sold to a new master, probably an Asiatic. Joseph was incorporated into this Asiatic civilization established as the occupying power in the Delta. It is important for these matters to be made clear, otherwise the whole story of Joseph and his sudden rise to power would seem hardly credible.

Joseph in the house of Potiphar, Pharaoh's eunuch

Joseph settled in Egypt, therefore, which for something like half a century[5] had been under Hyksos domination. The Semitic merchants who had bought him at Dothan resold him to an official of the court called Potiphar, *one of Pharaoh's officials and commander of the guard*. The name of Potiphar and his various titles have been very closely examined by Egyptologists intent on verifying the historical nature of the facts given by the Bible.

[5] The approximate dates of the Hyksos occupation of Egypt are 1720–1560 B.C.

Potiphar. Orientalists are still discussing even nowadays the composition of this name and the translation of its component elements. At least they are in agreement that these various elements have Egyptian roots.

One of Pharaoh's officials. Potiphar is commonly described as 'one of Pharaoh's eunuchs'. In fact the Egyptians seem to have felt a marked repugnance for those who were castrated. The eunuch as the guardian of the harem appears nowhere in the pharaonic documents. Nowadays historians are inclined to the view that, physiologically, Potiphar could not be regarded as a eunuch for the following reasons. Certainly in Mesopotamia eunuchs occupied a predominant position in the royal palaces, the most important administrative offices were reserved to them, and the monarch consulted them in council. There was nothing like that in Egypt. Yet it appears that by analogy with the Babylonian courts the title of eunuch was gratuitously attributed to the Pharaoh's important officials. Following a verbal fashion of foreign origin, at Memphis and at Thebes this strange title was adopted. In Egypt the word eunuch had thus come to designate quite simply a high official with an important function at the court of the Pharaoh.

Commander of the guard. This is the common translation. The view of J. Vergote, who himself adopts that of P. Montet, is that the meaning is 'officer of the mouth' and the root of the Hebrew word used on this occasion means 'cook'. At a later date the medieval royal courts provide examples of an analogous linguistic evolution: the former servant in charge of the stable took the name of constable (*comes stabuli,* the count of the stable); marshall and equerry or esquire are titles that have evolved in the same way.

So as a slave Joseph entered the service of Potiphar, an official of some Hyksos Pharaoh whose name has not come down to us. [6] Joseph had the good fortune to *lodge in the house of his Egyptian master* – in other words, he was not sent to be one of a team of agricultural workers engaged on the hard work of the fields. Joseph took after his shrewd father; it was not long before his keen intelligence and sensible opinions caused him to stand out. *Yahweh was with him,* Genesis tells us, and also *Yahweh made everything succeed that he turned his hand to*. Joseph's master soon understood that his slave was under the special protection of his tribal god. This in a short time earned Joseph the position of steward to the official. It was a small beginning but *Yahweh blessed the Egyptian's household out of consideration for Joseph; Yahweh's blessing extended to all his possessions, both household and estate*. As a result there was further promotion for Joseph who became the trusted servant of his master who *left Joseph to handle all his possessions, and with him at hand, concerned himself with nothing beyond the food he ate*.

In this story of Jacob's son exiled in Egypt we do not encounter any of those imposing and terrifying appearances with which Yahweh sometimes honoured his creature. Here there are no theophanies, no solemn reminders about the mission entrusted to the chosen one, no startling confirmation of the Covenant and the Promise. And yet Yahweh by no means left Joseph to his own devices, but acted in him and around him by the discreet and very various ways of Providence. This accounts for the profoundly human qualities of this part of the story, which is permeated by a veiled spirituality through which Yahweh's active concern can be per-

[6] Probably a member of the Apopi family. The great difficulty in discovering anything much about the history of the Hyksos arises from the fact that after the victory of the Egyptians over the Asiatic invaders (in about 1560 B.C., shortly before Joseph's death) the Pharaohs systematically destroyed the monuments, inscriptions and documents recalling this period of national disgrace.

ceived. At this point of the story it might be thought that the bad times were over; despite his status as a slave Joseph could now, it seemed, look with confidence to the future.

Further difficulties

From time to time, Yahweh's providential action, as is fitting, appears to us to have been almost visible. Consequently, Joseph's life was full of difficulties, dramatic events and a certain degree of confusion, all of which enabled Yahweh to rescue his servant from the most desperate of situations, and bestow on him the most unexpected and startling of rewards. All this, of course, occurred almost exclusively at the material level, the only one which a man of the seventeenth century B.C. could really understand. To speak to individuals or communities God can only use a language which they are capable of understanding. Thus we can see why Joseph's life appeared to be a series of ups and downs.

Under Yahweh's protection he led a happy life in his father's camp. He was sold by his brothers and was at once reduced to the dreadful condition of a slave. Under Yahweh's protection in the house of the Egyptian high official he rapidly succeeded in achieving promotion to the highest office open to a slave, and his master entrusted everything to him; he could well hope that all his heavy trials were over. Then, surprisingly, as the result of an odious accusation, he was thrown into prison.

It had to happen this way: the glory, power and loving kindness of Yahweh could then, on several occasions, be clearly manifested in an entirely unforeseen manner to preserve Joseph, Abraham's great grandson, from the malice of men, and on each occasion to advance him to an even higher and more successful position.

The incident is too well known for it to be repeated in detail here (Gen. 39: 7–20). Joseph's master's wife accused him of grossly insulting her by making indecent suggestions to her, whereas in reality it was the woman who made the advances, and Joseph rejected them. But the husband believed his wife and Joseph was thrown into prison.

There is a moral significance to this anecdote which should be noticed, since lessons of this kind are not very numerous in the history of the patriarchs. Joseph, Genesis tells us, *was well-built and handsome*. Custom afforded the legitimate wife great freedom, and Egyptian records show that she was regarded almost as the husband's equal. This was obviously quite different from the oriental custom of keeping wives far from the gaze of men. This social system, special to Egypt, left the way open on occasion to all sorts of abuse.

'How could I do anything so wicked,' Joseph answered his seducer, *'and sin against God?'* In this way the Bible warns young people against the sin into which they could be thoughtlessly led. It did not matter that Joseph's vehement refusal was the cause of so disastrous an outcome. The continuation of the story reveals that his scrupulous behaviour caused him to be imprisoned; he suffered cruel afflictions which were quite undeserved. But Yahweh was still at his side: Joseph went to prison as a slave, he came out again to be Pharaoh's counsellor.

Between the purchase of Joseph by the merchants and his arrival in Egypt there occurs a chapter belonging to the Yahwistic cycle which interrupts the story; it concerns Judah and his daughter-in-law Tamar (Gen. 38). It is a passage of relatively little interest to the modern reader.

A genealogical table of a typically oriental kind

explains how Judah, one of Jacob's sons, married a Canaanite woman. Yet it does provide a useful illustration of the profound difference of moral attitude between Joseph and Judah. After various incidents in which the levirate law [7] plays an essential part, it is surprising to observe the behaviour of Judah towards a 'sacred prostitute' (or someone giving herself out to be one). There is written evidence concerning these strange rites which were an integral part of Canaanite religion with its orgiastic ceremonies. In the neighbourhood of the temples of Baal and Ashtoreth 'holy' men and women (for such was the description given to these peculiar persons) offered themselves to passers-by with the intention of placing a portion of their remuneration in the temple treasury. Right from their nomadic period the Hebrews expressed their horror of these pagan customs; Abraham's descendants abhorred and cursed them.

To return to Joseph: the scabrous incident between Judah and Tamar when compared with Joseph's behaviour enables us to appreciate at its proper worth his moral value; he refused to betray his master's confidence and rejected the advances of the married woman, saying that he did not wish to sin against God. Here was a decided evolution in the human conscience.

---

[7] Levirate (from the Latin word *levir,* brother-in-law, and more especially, husband's brother); it was an ancient Semitic institution which is also found among other ancient peoples. If, in a family, the husband died without children his widow was obliged to marry, in order of age, her dead husband's brother (or other relation); in this way, the name and inheritance of the dead man would fall to the first son of this new union. If the second husband died without leaving a son the widow was obliged to marry the third brother, if there was one. This *levir,* the brother of the dead man, could not avoid the strange duty incumbent on him save by submitting to a humiliating ceremony: before the elders gathered together 'at the gate of the city' his brother's widow removed his sandal and spat in his face, saying at the the same time, 'That is what a man deserves who refuses to raise up his brother's house'. From that time the dwelling of the unworthy brother was known among the Israelites as the 'house of the unshod'. No doubt this dishonouring procedure was intended to reduce the number of those who might be tempted to avoid too easily a levirate marriage.

Joseph in prison: his two fellow-prisoners

Joseph's master, to avenge his honour, had him thrown in prison. There, shortly afterwards, two important court officials — the chief cup-bearer and the baker, with whom Pharaoh was very angry (Gen. 40) — were also incarcerated. The commander of the guard assigned Joseph to attend to them.[8]

Are the titles chief cup-bearer and chief baker really Egyptian? According to the specialists they are entirely accurate and there is documentary evidence for them in the papyri. Although at that period the Hyksos were masters of northern Egypt we can be sure that the court ceremonial of the dethroned Pharaohs was scrupulously preserved and applied by the military leaders of the invaders in their concern to appear as successors on the Egyptian throne of the old national dynasties.

Egyptian documents show that the cup-bearer was responsible for removing the earthenware stopper from the neck of the wine jar. In addition he had to taste the wine to make sure that it was of good quality. Having done so, he filled the king's cup and presented it to him with due ceremony. The baker, as the name implies, was in charge of the bakery and pastry-making, a department of great importance since the Egyptians were epicures and the Hyksos rulers endeavoured to copy their predecessors on this as on many other points. The names of thirty-eight kinds of pastry or cake and one hundred and fifty-seven kinds of bread have been preserved. Like

[8] The reader should bear in mind that in this chapter the scribe has combined two traditions, one Yahwistic and the other Elohistic. J tradition: Joseph, thrown in prison found himself in contact with two fellow prisoners, Egyptian officials who had fallen from royal favour. E tradition: Joseph, still steward of Potiphar's house, in the course of his duties, had to attend to two arrested courtiers while their case was being prepared, in the house of Potiphar, the commander of the guard. The modern reader should not be surprised at the somewhat erratic, not to say baffling, nature of the story. To give the explanation which follows a certain unity the Yahwistic tradition (that is, the prison story) has here been adopted because it is the most usual.

similar officials at the court of Louis XIV in France, these two Egyptian officials' positions were of the highest grade.

Dreams and their explanation

One morning while attending the two prisoners Joseph was surprised at their doleful faces. He asked them what was the matter. *'We have had a dream,'* they answered, *'but there is no one to interpret it.'* Something has already been said about dreams, but it concerned more especially the Semite nomads. Among the Egyptians the religious position was somewhat different. It is important to realize this since the science of dream interpretation was a primary factor in Joseph's political ascent, in the first place during the time of his captivity and then when he was summoned to the pharaoh's court.

According to Egyptian beliefs at this period sleep placed men in direct and real contact with the mysterious world in which the dead dwelt and where the gods reigned. It was concluded from this that dreams must be regarded as precious warnings and as indications of incomparable value for the conduct of daily life. Unfortunately, they often occurred in the form of allegories or symbols which were difficult to decipher, at least for ordinary people. Thus to discover the hidden meaning the necessity arose of consulting a specialist in the matter. So the gloom of the two imprisoned officials can be understood; each of them had experienced an odd dream and, as they remarked dolefully, *'there is no one to interpret it.'*

Not only did the Egyptians have manuals which, without danger of anachronism could be called 'Key to Dreams', they also had soothsayers who possessed the knowledge necessary to explain the images which had invaded the consciousness of the sleeper.

135

Joseph probably thought that he could derive some advantage from this situation. With the innate versatility of his race he asked these high-ranking officials to tell the reasons for their anxiety. *'Are not interpretations God's business?'* he was careful to remark, and then added, *'Come, tell me.'*

The cup-bearer spoke first. During the night he had seen a vine in front of him. *'On the vine there were three branches; no sooner had it budded than it blossomed, and its clusters became ripe grapes. I had Pharaoh's cup in my hand; I picked the grapes and squeezed them into Pharaoh's cup,* [9] *and put the cup into Pharaoh's hand.'*

The explanation of the dream seemed very simple to Joseph. *'The three branches,'* he explained, *'are three days. In another three days Pharaoh will release you and restore you to your place. Then you will hand Pharaoh his cup, as you did before, when you were his cup-bearer.'* Joseph then asked the cup-bearer on his release from prison to remember him as he was innocent of the crime for which he was blamed.

It was now the chief baker's turn. He too recounted his dream to the slave who seemed to be really clever in penetrating the secrets of the future. *'I too had a dream; there were three trays of cakes on my head. In the top tray there were all kinds of Pharaoh's favourite cakes, but the birds ate them off the tray on my head.'* Joseph's explanation was rather disappointing: *'The three trays are three days,'* he said. *'In another three days Pharaoh will release you and hang you on a gallows, and the birds will eat the flesh off your bones.'*

Events confirmed the truth of Joseph's predictions. But once restored to his charge the chief cup-bearer

[9] The operation described is similar to the preparation of grape juice, as it is now called. At that time it was done by squeezing a grape in the hand above a cup. It is curious to note that in some texts the title of cup-bearer is sometimes accompanied by the phrase 'with clean hands'. The reason can be well understood.

forgot his promise; or rather he forgot about the obscure Canaanite who had accurately foretold his release and return to favour. It is a common feature of social morality, noted incidentally by the scribe: the powerful of this world find it easy enough to forget the lowly who have rendered them assistance in difficult circumstances. Nevertheless, Yahweh was watching over his servant and did not abandon him.

Pharaoh's strange dreams: seven fat cows, seven lean cows

Two years after the chief cup-bearer's return to court (Gen. 41) Pharaoh had a dream, the well-known dream of the seven fat cows coming up from the Nile; but soon seven lean cows come up from the Nile and devour the seven fat cows. *Then Pharaoh awoke*. He fell asleep again and dreamed a second time. This time, seven ears of corn, *full and ripe* grew on the same stalk. Shortly afterwards, beside the first ears, grew seven ears which were *meagre and scorched by the east wind*.[10] *The scanty ears of corn swallowed the seven full and ripe ears of corn. Then Pharaoh awoke.*

At once on rising Pharaoh *had all the magicians and wise men of Egypt summoned to him* in order to obtain an authentic interpretation of his dream, but unfortunately none of them was able to supply the key to understanding them.

'Pharaoh,' says Genesis, or else 'Pharaoh, king of Egypt', always without the definite article. The Bible cannot be regarded as an historical work in the modern

[10] There is a geographical error here. In Egypt it is the south wind which dries and spoils the harvest thus causing famine. In Palestine it is the east wind (the Bible often mentions the wind from the south-east) coming from the desert. The story-teller or the scribe was mistaken in the correction that he made, interpreting with Palestine in mind.

sense of the term; these pages of Genesis are intended to relate the dramatic adventures of the clan of Abraham and his descendants, the nomad patriarchs, the envoys of the one God. The Old Testament was never meant to furnish us with the complicated history of the Near East in ancient times.

Yet it is interesting to note that this term Pharaoh was used in the Bible while in the West its precise meaning was unknown. It needed the archaeological discoveries of last century and especially the deciphering of the hieroglyphics for the historical meaning of this term to be obtained. Nowadays orientalists have even discovered its etymology: *pr-'a,* literally the 'great house'. At the time of the Old Empire (2780–2280) the term designated the palace buildings, then, as a result of the evolution of the language it came to mean the court and, finally, it was taken as a synonym for the sovereign, 'for he alone in the world possesses a palace' (*pr-'a*).

In the biblical text the reader will have noticed that the name of the Pharaoh in Joseph's time is not mentioned. On this account certain scholars have come to the conclusion that the account is not historical. Some eminent Egyptologists have pointed out, however, that at the beginning of the New Empire (1560), which came immediately after the period of the occupation by the Hyksos, the title of Pharaoh by itself was in agreement with the practice of the Egyptian scribes. The actual name of the Pharaoh, completing his royal title, did not appear until much later, at least in the papyri, at the late period and during Greco-Roman times. This does not apply, of course, to inscriptions on the pedestals of statues.

Another expression used by the writer of the narrative seems to indicate that the dream depicted the incident of the seven fat and seven lean cows in the delta of the Nile, that is, in the very heart of the territory conquered by the Hyksos. [11]

According to the translation by E. Dhorme the passage in question should read that the cows were feeding 'among the rushes in the marshland'. Now from certain Egyptian texts we know that ever since the Old Empire (2780–2280) the marshes of the delta, with their dense vegetation of rushes and papyrus, provided an ideal feeding ground for herds of cattle. Pharaoh's dream, therefore, certainly appears to have had as its setting the Delta in which the Hyksos were settled.

Joseph interprets Pharaoh's dreams

Without losing sight of Joseph's story, it will be useful for the moment to examine the social and religious standing of the 'wise men' summoned by Pharaoh to interpret his two successive dreams. What exactly were these 'wise men', these 'magicians' (*hartummim*) mentioned by the Bible whom, as we shall see, Joseph was to cover with confusion by his enlightening explanation?

The identification of this caste of interpreters of dreams is a recent discovery in Egyptology, so that we now know that around the sovereign, from morning to night, there was a body of priests called 'scribes of the House of Life'. Before taking up their posts they had studied for a long time in a religious school in which they learnt everything to do with magic and the control of occult powers. From the first hours of the day they surrounded

[11] In fact, on several occasions the Hyksos pharaohs attempted to advance to the south in the valley of the Nile; the stupendous agricultural wealth of this long corridor was a constant temptation to them. Some Hyksos incursions penetrated as far as Thebes, the capital of Upper Egypt where the 'barbarians of the north' as the natives called them, contrived to settle for some time. In any case, southern Egypt, freed from the Hyksos occupation, was rapidly transformed into a centre of active resistance against the invaders; and it was there that arose the military and national movement which finally drove out the Hyksos.

the king, they assisted him in his ritual toilet, they were not far from the table when he ate, they were in his bed chamber when he retired. The pharaoh, a son of the gods and a god himself, was continually protected in all the actions of his earthly life, by a watchful band of magicians, men in possession of important occult knowledge. These were the 'magicians and wise men' mentioned by the Bible and whose description is to be found in the papyrus.

But no one could interpret [his dream] *for Pharaoh.* That is, there was no one among these experts able to do so. In this disturbing situation the chief cup-bearer remembered the young Hebrew in the prison who had surprisingly revealed the future to him. He told his master about it and an order was at once given for Joseph to be brought to the palace. In true oriental style Joseph wore a beard and, in accordance with the custom of Egyptians of the lower classes, his only garment was a loin cloth. This was entirely unsuitable dress for an audience. *Joseph shaved and changed his clothes, and came into Pharaoh's presence.*

Notice how at the beginning of the conversation Joseph reveals his religious attitude. *'I do not count,'* he said. *'It is God who will give Pharaoh a favourable answer.'* The problem was explained to him and he at once provided an answer: the seven fat cows represented seven years of fine harvests; the seven lean cows symbolized seven years of terrible famine which would follow the period of plenty. The prophecy was entirely confirmed by the second dream which was a repetition of the first using a similar allegory. This double dream proved that the event was *already determined by God, and God is impatient to bring it about.*

At this Joseph, who after all was only a slave of little importance, ventured to give good advice to his sovereign.

140

He did so very cleverly and with a great affectation of humility, asking nothing for himself, of course, and his advice seemed absolutely disinterested. *'Pharaoh should now choose a man who is intelligent and wise to govern the land of Egypt. Pharaoh should take action. . . .'* Immediately Joseph placed before Pharaoh a plan to be carried out with all urgency: during the seven years of abundance a tax should be imposed on the farmers of one fifth of their harvests. Then, by government authority,

A corn granary in Egypt (tomb painting, *c*. 1460 B.C.)

these reserves should be stored carefully in certain urban centres; by this means, when the periods of scarcity came, the country could be saved from famine.

Both Pharaoh's dreams and Joseph's far-seeing plan fit in very accurately with the agricultural fluctuations of the valley of the Nile. The whole life of Egypt depends essentially on the annual flooding of the Nile. Pliny, the Latin author, explains the position by means of a table which is eloquent in its simplicity:

12 cubits (at Aswan, where the level of the Nile was measured); famine.

14 cubits: joy.   15 cubits: delight.

On the other hand, if the rise was too great it meant disaster in the shape of dykes carried away, irrigation systems disorganized and, when the river went down, since the water subsided too slowly, it was impossible to sow at the proper time. Egyptologists who have made a careful examination of the biblical account of Joseph have sought to discover if the two periods – seven years of plenty followed by seven years of scarcity – are recorded in Egyptian history. So far no trace of them has been found. Generally speaking biblical scholars consider that in this case the number seven has a symbolical value: $3 + 4$ (4, the earth, a square; 3, heaven, a triangle); the sum, 7, being the Universe or, at least, a figure of a certain allegorical significance.

A slave who suddenly becomes viceroy of Egypt

The failure of Pharaoh's official wisemen and magicians to provide at once an accurate interpretation, together with the explanation offered by Joseph, a former Canaanite shepherd summoned straight from prison, who in addition, like a professional soothsayer, had suggested an immediate plan to save the country, all combined to make Pharaoh conceive a certain admiration for the young Hebrew who appeared to be inspired by his tribal god. Undoubtedly this was of interest to Pharaoh, even though he did not worship a strange god; a polytheist was always ready to accept benefits from whatever higher power they emanated. Joseph had scarcely concluded his prophecy, embellished with judicious advice, when Pharaoh exclaimed, *'Can we find any man like this, possessing the spirit of God?'*

Without more ado, since the interests of the country required it, Pharaoh decided to raise Joseph the slave to the highest office. And, in fact, such a sudden elevation was by no means unusual in oriental countries. There are several examples of it in Egyptian history, and the Bible itself, though at a much later period, relates the unexpected good fortune of Daniel in not dissimilar circumstances.

Careful reading of this chapter of Genesis shows that Joseph received the two different titles of master of the palace or chancellor (Egyptian documents call it 'Master of the house of Pharaoh') and that of viceroy or governor (some Egyptologists prefer the use of the term *Vizier*). All are agreed that these were offices of the highest degree.

In addition the scene of Joseph's investiture is very accurately reported by Genesis, as is proved by mural paintings: those, for example, adorning the tomb of Rekhmire, or those of which the vizier Rameses is the hero. *Pharaoh took the ring from his hand and put it on Joseph's*. This was a symbolical action ratifying the delegation of powers. The ring in question on which the royal seal was engraved, enabled Joseph to authenticate the acts of government. All these details are historically correct. In ancient times, officials, as indeed private individuals, used two sorts of seal: there was the Babylonian seal in cylindrical form, with the seal carved on the surface, which was worn hanging from the neck, and also in the form of a stone set in a ring. According to the archaeologists at the time of Joseph (end of the seventeenth century B.C.) the Egyptians almost exclusively used the ring seal, as the Bible relates. The gold chain which Pharaoh placed round Joseph's neck, despite the doubts of some Egyptologists on the point, may be regarded as a ritual gesture forming part of the traditional ceremonies of investiture. All these details related in the Bible are in surprising agreement with the findings of archaeology.

A further interesting detail of ritual was that at once on his appointment Joseph was clothed in fine linen. The Hebrew word here used by the Bible means linen cloth of high quality, a characteristic Egyptian product. This involved a second change of clothes for Joseph (not to be confused with the clean garment put on the prisoner when he was summoned from prison). This new garment, woven from royal linen, was one of the external signs of the office of vizier.

Another typically Egyptian detail was that Pharaoh made Joseph *ride in the best chariot he had after his own, and they cried before him 'Abrek',* that is, 'Beware' or 'Make way'. It is very probable that this was shouted by heralds galloping before Pharaoh's chariot, or even, on occasion, before the chariot of certain high officials. There is a scene of this kind depicted in the hypogeum of Neferhotep in which the heralds clear the way as the chariot goes forward.

At this time Joseph must have been about thirty. According to the tradition of the country, officials of Syrian or Palestinian origin were given a new name which was Egyptian. A papyrus of the thirteenth dynasty provides an example of this custom: opposite the foreign names, and facing the name of the offices occupied, the scribe has carefully noted the name given to the officials by their new country. Thus by Pharaoh's order, Joseph the Hebrew became Zaphenath-paneah. Orientalists recognize it as an Egyptian form. Fr de Vaux in the Jerusalem Bible translates it by *God says: he is living.*

Soon afterwards we find the new vizier marrying a woman of the nobility named Asenath, the daughter of Potiphera (not to be confused with Potiphar, the official mentioned at the beginning of the narrative) who was high-priest of the city of On (later Heliopolis, a religious centre to the north of Memphis). According to some orientalists Asenath means 'belonging to the goddess Neith' (a sort of Minerva of the banks of the Nile).

Potiphera ('Gift of Ra') is a characteristic name of the Delta region.

Joseph's agrarian policy

In the northern part of Egypt Joseph was now to all intents and purposes the food controller. His predictions were fulfilled one by one. First came seven years of plenty, the rise of the Nile taking place perfectly satisfactorily; as a result of copious rain in the tropical regions the Nile and its tributaries were well supplied with water and the consequent flooding covered the whole valley of the river with black mud on which, in spring time and afterwards, heavy crops were grown. During this period of plenty the people gave vent to their joy, thanking the Nile god. In his honour they sang praises to the 'Creator of wheat', to the 'Maker of barley', for 'he made everything that is good' and he was regarded as the 'Lord of all pleasing foods'.

The new food controller did not share the general euphoria. He regarded these few years of plenty merely as a respite which was to be used to the best advantage. At the end of each harvest the government stored vast quantities of cereals, and Joseph was careful that these stocks should be kept in specially fitted barns which were thief-proof. The architectural style of these barns is known to us; in Egyptian tombs archaeologists have discovered various representations of these buildings, and in the Louvre Museum, for example, there is an earthenware model of one.

The writer of the account in Genesis was, of course, an oriental scribe; on this occasion he has allowed himself to be carried away by his enthusiasm. *Joseph,* he tells us, *stored the corn like the sand of the sea, so much that they stopped reckoning, since it was beyond all estimating.* We should not take this too literally; the Hyksos were

145

far too Egyptianized not to have adopted the old bureaucratic traditions of the country in which cautious accountants never missed an opportunity of drawing up lists with ingoings and outgoings carefully noted.

After seven years of plenty a terrible period of drought began in the region of the great African lakes. As a result the rise of the river in the valley on the Nile was manifestly insufficient and despite the system of channels devised to ensure the distribution of water the land remained infertile. Very soon famine loomed. The people came to Pharaoh, pleading their distress and asking for bread. Pharaoh sent them to Joseph, the minister in charge and distributor of cereals.

Unexpected family reunion

In Canaan, also, the sun burnt up the harvest and the pasture. In Hebron, Jacob's clan began to be seriously concerned about future food supplies. News travels quickly; it did so especially in the ancient East, and Jacob very soon learned that in the Egyptian delta the Hyksos government, with considerable reserves in hand, was selling off its surplus stocks of wheat and barley. *'Go down,'* said Jacob, *'and buy grain for us there, that we may survive and not die.'* There was no time to be lost. With a herd of donkeys to bring back the sacks of cereals the ten brothers set out. In no time at all they had come up with the long line of starving Canaanites who were also on their way to the banks of the Nile.

Joseph's important position obliged him to superintend the commercial transactions which were extremely advantageous to the Egyptian treasury. He had to take charge of those who were responsible for counting the bushels sold, he supervised the receipt of the precious metals received in payment; he inspected the accounts of the scribes. It should be remembered that Egypt was

Jacob's sons must have journeyed to Egypt like this.

one of the most bureaucratic countries imaginable.

Suddenly he saw a group of Asiatics arriving whom he was able to identify at once. It was ten of his brothers, those who had sold him so deliberately to the slave merchants. According to the rules of etiquette the ten foreigners bowed down to the ground before the vizier. It was hardly possible for Joseph not to be reminded then of the two dreams that he had been foolish enough to tell his brothers. There was the first dream about the ten sheaves carried by his brothers which bowed down before Joseph's sheaf. Then there was the dream in which he saw the stars behaving in the same fashion. Now, having become an important official of Pharaoh's court he found himself all at once the object of his own family's respect. It was an unexpected realization of his childhood's dreams.

Dressed in his fine robes as vizier Joseph was not recognized by his brothers, and he was careful not to say who he was. When the little group came before him he adopted a very severe attitude and, pretending not to understand their language, conversed with them through an interpreter. To their great surprise Jacob's sons found themselves accused of belonging to a spy network and of having come to Egypt on the pretext of buying wheat, but in reality to discover the weak points in the fortifications. The Israelites protested; they were, they explained by way of justification, twelve brothers; one of them had died long ago and the youngest, whose name was Benjamin, had been obliged to remain in Canaan with their old father, the head of the clan. Joseph, who had already made up his mind what he would do, declared that he could not believe such a story. He ordered them to be put in prison.

After three days there the ten brothers appeared again before the vizier. There was further, severe questioning.

Joseph then laid down his conditions: one of them was to remain in prison in Egypt; the nine others would be allowed to return to Canaan with the quantity of corn which they said that they needed. The prisoner would not be set free until the return of the caravan to Egypt bringing with it the youngest brother (that is, Benjamin). In this way, the vizier declared that he could be convinced of the truthfulness of their statements. If they did not accept these conditions they should prepare to die.

The perplexity of Jacob's sons was obvious. In Joseph's presence, and unaware that he understood perfectly all that they were saying, they began to complain aloud. *'Truly,'* they said, *'we are being called to account for our brother. We saw his misery of soul when he begged our mercy, but we did not listen to him and now this misery has come home to us.'* Reuben reproached his brothers bitterly: *'Did I not tell you not to wrong the boy? But you did not listen, and now we are brought to account for his blood.'* As if he did not understand what they were saying, Joseph remained seemingly unconcerned, but after a minute or two, overcome by emotion he was obliged to withdraw from them: *'he left them and wept'*, says Genesis. But this did not prevent his carrying out his plan in every detail. He gave orders for Simeon to be bound and taken off to prison. With heavy hearts the band of nine brothers set out on the way back to Canaan.

Jacob's despair

The first stage of the return journey (Gen. 42: 25–28) took them past the line of fortresses protecting the frontier and as far as the beginning of the sandy wilderness of Zin. On the evening of the first day they halted to pitch camp for the night. One of them, opening the provision sack to feed his donkey, discovered on top of the corn a purse containing the money [1] [2] which he had given to the Egyptian collector. Shortly afterwards each one of the brothers also found in a sack of corn the money paid for the purchases of wheat. It all seemed inexplicable. They could hardly have guessed that this little scene had been arranged by the severe vizier whom they had just left. Their anxiety can be understood. *Their hearts sank, and they looked at one another in panic, saying, 'What is this that God has done to us?'* Obviously it was no bad thing that they should feel the hand of God weighing upon them.

On their arrival at Hebron they hastened to relate to their father, point by point, all their extraordinary adventures. They told him that for Simeon, kept as a hostage in Pharaoh's prison, to be set free they had to take their youngest brother Benjamin to the formidable vizier in order to prove to him that they had not lied.

Jacob protested at once. His son Joseph had been devoured by a wild beast (or so, at least, he thought). Simeon was imprisoned in a foreign land. And now it was a question of risking Benjamin's life with a journey which would surely prove dangerous. A long discussion ensued. In the end Jacob categorically refused to do what his sons requested. Benjamin was not to go to Egypt. *'If any harm came to him on the journey you are to undertake,'* declared Jacob, *'you would send me down to Sheol with my white head bowed in grief.'*

That was all very well, but the fearful drought which, in the previous year had burnt up all the pasture, continued, causing acute famine (Gen. 43). To prevent the situation growing worse it would be necessary to return

---

[1] [2] During the second intermediary period (corresponding with the Hyksos occupation) the legal weight used for transactions was the *deben* (91 grammes). At that period business was conducted almost exclusively with silver. On this account, in the Egyptian language the word 'silver' became a synonym for currency. It is this same word which is used in the biblical passage quoted.

to Egypt for a further purchase of corn. That was the general opinion and Jacob agreed with it. But his sons refused to 'go down'[13] again to Egypt if they were not allowed to take with them their young brother Benjamin whose presence had been required by the vizier. Once again there was a heated argument, and cries of despair from Jacob. At last, he found himself bound to accept the separation from his son: *'Take your brother,'* he said, *'and go back to the man.'* He could hardly have supposed that this 'man' was Joseph his beloved son.

Before leaving Hebron they decided to take back to Egypt the money found so unexpectedly in the sacks of corn. They supposed that it was a mistake on the part of the scribes at the time of payment. In addition, in order to receive a kindly welcome, they would take the vizier gifts of those Canaanite specialities of which Egyptians were fond – a little balsam, gum tragacanth and resin; to these more usual products they decided to add a little honey, pistachio nuts and almonds. Obviously they knew how to curry favour with foreign officials.

Jacob's ten sons set out again for the Delta. At Hebron the old patriarch, alone with his womenfolk, was torn by grief. He did not suspect that Yahweh was watching over him and was soon to give him one of the most exciting moments of his life.

The ten brothers before Joseph

Directly on arrival in Egypt Jacob's ten sons presented themselves in the audience chamber and bowed low before the viceroy (Gen. 43: 15–34). At his first glance Joseph noticed Benjamin, who was, like himself, Rachel's son. Doing his best to hide his emotion he ordered his chamberlain to take the small party to his

---

[13] From the Judah massif there is a gradual descent down to the lower plains of the Delta.

own house. He spoke in the language of the country (which his brothers did not understand) and added that they were to eat with him.

Seeing that without explanation they were being taken in a new direction Joseph's brothers began to be afraid. Were they being taken to prison, they wondered, for having carried off the sacks of corn without paying for them? To the best of their ability they explained to the chamberlain, telling him of their surprise at the discovery of the purses when they opened their sacks, and they made it clear that they had felt obliged to bring back to the Egyptian government this money which did not belong to them. The chamberlain reassured them: *'Do not be afraid,'* he said, *'your God and your father's God has put a treasure in your corn-sacks. Your money reached me safely.'* The whole matter seemed to become increasingly obscure. At this point the chamberlain brought them Simeon who had just been released from prison.

The brothers' donkeys were given fodder, and water was brought for the travellers so that, in accordance with eastern custom, after a long journey they could wash their feet. Before them they saw a table on which were arranged the presents which they had brought from Canaan.

Joseph then came in. The Hebrews bowed low. He conversed with them familiarly. *'Is your father well, the old man you told me of? Is he still alive?'* They replied that he was well. Once more they knelt before Joseph, bowing down to the ground. *'Is this your youngest brother,'* Joseph went on, pointing to Benjamin, *'of whom you told me?'* It was a dramatic moment. To hide his tears Joseph was obliged hurriedly to leave and go to his own room where he wept. After bathing his face he returned to his brothers and made them sit down according to their rank, from the eldest to the youngest.

They were amazed: for how could Pharaoh's minister know the order of their birth?

Joseph did not sit with his guests; a special table was set for him facing that of his brothers. *For,* Genesis informs us, *Egyptians cannot take food with Hebrews; they have a horror of it.* Some historians have seen this as an example of the marked antipathy of the Egyptians for foreigners. Indeed dislike of foreigners is usual in the Near East, nowadays as formerly. But the special arrangement of the banqueting hall in which Joseph and his brothers were gathered together is to be explained rather by ritual requirements. For Egyptians and Hebrews do not agree about which are the unclean animals — those, that is, whose flesh cannot be eaten. Moreover, even in the valley of the Nile itself, these prohibitions differed from place to place. In one, the flesh of some animal, bird or fish was allowed and in the neighbouring district it would be prohibited. The explanation is to be found, in fact, in ancestral memories of ancient totemistic traditions. In the present case, on the occasion of a meal taken in common between Arameans and an Egyptian official, it was necessary to have different dishes [14] served, of course, at different tables.

The conclusion of this part of the story seems to reveal in Joseph a cruel tendency, and it is almost tempting to suppose that while he had achieved the position of a high Egyptian official he retained in the bottom of his heart a desire to be avenged for what he had endured fifteen years previously. By no means. The remainder of the story furnishes proofs of his magnanimous nature and sometimes of the delicacy of feeling that he displayed.

Jacob's sons set off rejoicing on their way back to

[14] By force of circumstances certain dishes were suitable both for Egyptians and Hebrews, since at one moment *he had portions carried to his brothers from his own dish.*

Hebron, urging on before them the donkeys laden with sacks of corn. All seemed to have turned out well, or so they thought. They did not know what the immediate future had in store for them. For Joseph had told his chamberlain secretly to slip into Benjamin's sack a fine cup which Joseph used for drinking and for reading omens.[15] In accordance with a carefully laid plan the Hebrew party was allowed to leave the city, but shortly afterwards a threatening troop of guards under the orders of the chamberlain came up with them and ordered them to halt. The chamberlain accused the Hebrews of behaving very badly after the kind welcome that had been given them; on leaving the viceroy's house they had found nothing better to do than to carry off his cup. They were amazed at the accusation. The chamberlain told them clearly that the thief would pay dearly for his unscrupulous behaviour.

Strong in their innocence the brothers hastened to open their sacks. The Egyptian guards had received orders to begin their search with the eldest, and the methodical examination seemed to produce no result. Finally they came to Benjamin's sack and, almost as if by chance, the cup was found. The brothers were

[15] Scripture scholars have been much puzzled by this mysterious cup which Joseph used to drink from and to read omens. It was a typically Egyptian ritual object, used in the valley of the Nile by the soothsayers whose office it was to read the future. This particular sort of magic is a form of lecanomancy: the cup was filled with water and a few drops of oil were poured on it: contemplation of the shapes formed by the oil provoked a sort of hypnotic state in the medium who then saw (or so he said) the faces of persons or silhouettes of objects enabling him to foretell future events. It was not unlike fortune-telling by reading the tea leaves in a cup or the use of a crystal ball. Is it true that Joseph the Aramean, who had lived for more than fifteen years in the Egyptianized milieu of the Hyksos, had become a specialist in this sort of magic? It is difficult to believe it. For this 'science' was the function of a circle of initiates who had followed a lengthy course of training. And it is improbable that Joseph's duties as controller of the food of the whole country would have left him sufficient time to concern himself with magic, at least in the religious schools. Thus modern biblical scholars are fairly well agreed that from the context Joseph must have boasted to his brothers that he possessed certain super-normal powers; it was a further opportunity to make them even more afraid of him.

speechless. There could be no doubt about it: Yahweh's anger was upon them, and it was obviously the punishment for the crime that they had formerly committed, by common agreement, on the person of Joseph. The blow was nonetheless terrible.

The chamberlain, who had received instructions from Joseph, told them that the guilty one, Benjamin, would be kept in Egypt as a slave. The other members of the party were authorized to continue their journey to Canaan. At once the ten brothers conferred together. It was impossible for them to return to their father without bringing with them Benjamin, his beloved son, the joy of his old age. As a mark of their despair they tore their clothes. Instead of going on towards Hebron they decided to return to the city where they asked to be received in audience by the vizier. Brought before him *they fell on the ground before him*. As he looked at them he remembered the details of his premonitory dream — everything was turning out as the dream of the sheaves of corn had foretold.

The somewhat dramatic exchange opened with a short but sharp accusation from Joseph. There followed a long and pathetic plea from Judah, a real masterpiece which is one of the finest passages in the Old Testament. Judah painted a moving picture of the situation. He explained to the viceroy (whom he was far from recognizing as his brother Joseph) that their old father Jacob, who had stayed in Hebron in his shepherd's tent, had entrusted them with Benjamin, his youngest son, only after much hesitation. The patriarch had suffered a grievous loss by the death of one of his sons named Joseph. If the caravan were now to return to the camp without Benjamin it would be a terrible blow for the patriarch, who would die of grief. Judah concluded by offering that if the vizier would be pleased to free Benjamin, he, Judah, would take the place of his young brother and become the vizier's slave: *'Let the boy go back with his brothers. How indeed could I go back to my father and not have the boy with me? I could not bear to see the misery that would overwhelm my father.'*

Dramatic sequel

As Judah came to an end of his speech Jacob's sons endeavoured to read the verdict in their judge's eyes. But he merely gave a brief order for all the Egyptians present to withdraw and for the doors to be shut. His brothers then saw him leave his seat and, his face bathed in tears, come slowly towards them. His voice broken with sobs he told them, *'I am Joseph!'* And he went on to ask anxiously, *'Is my father really still alive?'*

It was a moving scene. The Israelites, who had undergone a severe ordeal stood rooted to the spot with emotion. And also with fear; revenge, as they well knew, was the rule among Semitic peoples, and the law of retaliation was always strictly applied in the name of justice. And now they, the ten guilty men, weak and disarmed, were at the mercy of him whom they had once sold to the slave merchant. It was useless for them to delude themselves; it was now their turn to experience the horrors of slavery, the time of their punishment had come. But Joseph did not call the guards. On the contrary he held out his arms, saying in a kindly voice, *'Come closer to me'*.

In the face of his brothers' terrified reaction Joseph felt obliged to give them some explanation. They had nothing to fear, he told them, they could rely on his feelings of deep affection. As a religious man, and as a generous one too, he described his adventure. At Dothan, when they threw him into the tank, and then when they sold him to the Midianite merchants, they thought to satisfy their hatred, but they were wrong. Their behaviour was provoked by Yahweh himself. They thought to rid themselves of him for ever by selling him to the slave dealers. In fact it was through the agency of the ten brothers that Yahweh himself 'sent him before' to the banks of the Nile with the obvious purpose, which had now appeared clearly to all; as he had become viceroy he was now in a position at this tragic time to save the clan from death and almost certain extinction.

The brothers remained as if stunned. Joseph continued his speech. As a man of action he had rapidly evolved a plan. The frightful period of drought which pressed so heavily over the land for the past two years had still five years to run. It was too dangerous for the Hebrew encampment to remain in its tents at Hebron in a situation far remote from the Egyptian sources of supply. Consequently the brothers should return to their father's camp and persuade him to come as quickly as possible and settle in the Delta near the wheat barns put up by Pharaoh's government. Thus Jacob's family would be completely reunited. By enjoying Joseph's protection they would be certain of an easy life; in addition he would see that they were given the best pasture in the land. *'You shall live,'* he said, *'in the land of Goshen.'*

Before he began to speak Joseph had ordered that the doors should be closed. But outside, and despite the thickness of the panels, men were listening. The viceroy had been heard to sob and his words were carefully noted. Without a moment's delay the details of this eventful scene were reported to Pharaoh. And when, shortly afterwards, Joseph approached his sovereign to inform him of the news (which he already knew) Pharaoh readily agreed to Joseph's clan settling in Egypt.

Jacob and all his family go to Egypt

Joseph's eleven brothers set out again for the land of Canaan. It was an imposing caravan: there was a herd of donkeys laden with sacks of corn and presents for the patriarch; there were beasts of burden with the provisions necessary for Jacob's approaching journey, and Egyptian waggons to transport the wives and children across the sandy or stony plains of Paran and Zin between the Negeb and the Delta.

On their arrival at Hebron Jacob's sons told him the glad and wonderful news: *'Joseph is still alive. Indeed it is he who is administrator of the whole land of Egypt.'*[16] The old man, who in the first part of his life as a shepherd had frequently tricked his fellows, refused to believe the news. But he was soon obliged to yield before the evidence, the rich presents and sumptuous gifts sent by his son, whom he had believed lost for ever.

For nomads the move from Hebron to the borders of the Delta, a mere 220 miles of travelling, presented no difficulties. The tents were folded and the baggage was loaded on the donkeys. Sons and grandsons, wives and concubines, were not long in setting off; they were accompanied, of course, by the throng of servants, slaves, and shepherds whose responsibility it was to lead the flocks. In short, the whole establishment took the road to Mizraim, as the Semites called the land of Egypt.

A halt was called at Beersheba, the sacred spot where formerly Abraham had camped. At a later date Isaac too had dwelt there for a time. And it was from here, it will be remembered, that, after his serious disagreement with Esau, Jacob left for Haran in Upper Mesopotamia to go to his uncle Laban. Beersheba was the obvious place to

---

[16] Not the whole, only that part contained within the Delta, but by no means an insignificant part.

halt; it enabled Jacob to offer a sacrifice to God. In answer God appeared to the patriarch; he enjoined on his chosen one to continue the journey to Egypt when his descendants would become *a great nation*. In addition he told Jacob that his son Joseph's hand should close his eyes.

Establishment of the Hebrew clan in the land of Goshen

Informed of the approach of his family Joseph took his chariot and went out to meet his father. The meeting was a touching one. Shortly afterwards, through Joseph's good offices, Jacob was officially presented to Pharaoh who received him with special kindness, giving orders that his minister's relations should be assured the very best living conditions. But where was the Hebrew camp established?

In the land of Goshen, according to the topographical details given on several occasions[17] by Joseph (Yahwistic tradition); *'In the best region of the land, namely the land of Rameses',* Pharaoh ordered (Priestly tradition).[18]

Once again we have two discordant versions which, as usual, the scribe has not been concerned to harmonize. The arguments between scholars may well be imagined but now the problem seems to be settled. It is thought that the Hyksos Pharaohs allowed the Israelites to settle in the Wadi Tumilat region (see map, p. 160). Geographi-

---

[17] *'You shall live in the country of Goshen,'* Joseph informs Jacob through Judah (Gen. 45: 10). *Joseph had his chariot made ready and went up to meet his father Israel in Goshen* (Gen. 46: 29). *'You will be able to stay in the land of Goshen'* (Gen. 46: 34). *'My father and brothers . . . are now in the land of Goshen,'* Joseph told Pharaoh in speaking of the members of his tribe (Gen. 47: 1).

[18] *'I will give you the best land of Egypt offers, and you shall feed on the fat of the land'* — it is Pharaoh who is speaking — (Gen. 45: 18). *Joseph gave them a holding in the land of Egypt, and in the best region of the land, namely the land of Rameses, according to Pharaoh's command* (Gen. 47: 11).

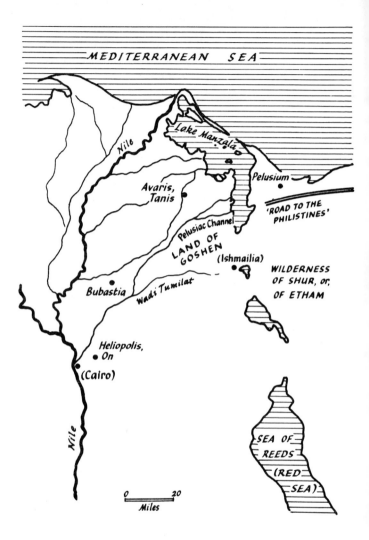

THE EASTERN DELTA OF THE NILE
showing the Land of Goshen

cal information about this region will not be out of place here.

To begin with it must be explained why the Bible speaks of the land of Rameses. This is an anachronism, though almost an excusable one. A fair number of the Israelites, but at a much later period, did dwell in the land of Rameses, that is in the region near Avaris which was for a time the Hyksos' capital.[19] The Israelites, or at least some of them, had been deported there by the Egyptian national forces after the expulsion of the Hyksos, and had been obliged to work as slaves on the profane and religious buildings put up to the glory of Rameses II. It was from this 'land of Rameses' that the Israelites left for their Exodus in about 1200 under the leadership of Moses — as we shall see in the next volume.

It can be well understood how the name of this 'land of Rameses', the accursed country, remained fixed in the ancestral memory of the Israelites, while through a very human psychological process they gradually forgot the existence of the land of Goshen where, free and happy, they had lived for several centuries right at the beginning of their Egyptian adventure.

The land of Goshen (or Gessen as some writers spell it) was very suitable for a clan engaged in sheep rearing. It was a rather unusual kind of steppe land extending to the east from the easternmost branch of the Nile (the Pelusiac branch) between the last branch of the river and the line of lakes (Bahlia and the Bitter Lakes). The region could be regarded as a kind of no-man's-land separating the Delta from the wilderness. As was said above it was in a particular corner — the Wadi Tumilat — that Jacob's

[19] In succession this city bore the names of Hotuarit (of which the Greeks made Avaris), of Pi-Rameses (under the Rameses — 1300–1100), and lastly of Tanis.

family settled. Along the whole length of this wadi, nowadays occupied by the canal connecting the Pelusiac branch with Lake Timsah, excavators have found traces of a channel supplied by the Nile which at the time of the Pharaohs enabled this little valley to be flooded every year (June to September). The Tumilat steppe which had originally been infertile changed in the autumn into fertile cultivated land. Of course, the owners of the flocks took their sheep to the nearby pastures which were not reached by the flooding.

We possess interesting information on the subject of the agricultural wealth of the Wadi Tumilat derived from the violent recriminations of the Israelites when they were very dissatisfied (to say the least) at the interminable stay imposed on them by Moses in the dry harsh plain of Sinai. The Book of Numbers relates a series of protests revealing a somewhat disquieting spirit of revolt. *'Think of the fish we used to eat free in Egypt,'* they complained, *'the cucumbers, melons, leeks, onions and garlic!'* Further on we discover in the same book, and for the same reasons, their fond memories of the land of Goshen where they had only to sow in order to harvest and where figs, wine and pomegranates grew. To maintain the courage of the people marching in the Sinai wilderness Moses spoke of the Promised Land and told them of their entry soon into a land where milk and honey flowed (Exod. 3: 8, 17). But he was careful to tell the Hebrews that they were not to count on finding in Canaan so wonderful a land as Goshen: *'For the land which you are to enter and make your own is not like the land of Egypt from which you came, where you sowed your seed and watered it by tread* [with a water wheel, a primitive apparatus operated by foot and used to raise the irrigation water from the streams] *like a vegetable garden'* (Deut. 11: 10).

Although this part of the Delta should not be regarded as the best land of Egypt (to repeat Pharaoh's exaggerated description) it is obvious that in the eyes of these Arameans, obliged to go from pasture to pasture in search of grass which only too often proved to be burnt up by the sun, the land of Goshen in general and the Wadi Tumilat in particular rapidly came to be regarded almost as a sort of fairy land.

In this frontier province, a little apart from the life of Egypt, Joseph's tribe was able to increase and multiply in comfort. And this geographical situation away from the important centres enabled Israel to remain shepherds, for they were gardeners or farmers only from time to time. In addition, as Maspero pertinently remarks, in this corner of the country, isolated from the principal manifestations of Egyptian civilization, 'the Hebrews did not leave the God of their fathers to bow down before the triads and enneads of the Egyptians'.

At this point the scribe, drawing on the Priestly code (which always emphasizes the genealogical factor), inserted a list of the names of Israel's sons who went to Egypt with the Patriarch Jacob. Together with Joseph and the two sons[20] that he had at this time by his wife Asenath, the number of Jacob's male descendants amounted to seventy.

Joseph, a very clever minister

Without doubt Pharaoh had made a fortunate choice: his food controller was also a first-rate financial expert. When the first year of scarcity began the Egyptians came

---

[20] At the time of the arrival of Jacob's caravan in the land of Goshen, Joseph had two sons by his wife Asenath, Manasseh (*'he has made me forget,'* that is, God has made me forget my sorrow and all my father's family) and Ephraim (*'he has made me fruitful'* to which must be added *'in the land of my misfortune'*).

to ask the government to provide them with a little grain lest they starve. According to Genesis, it appears that in return for the corn Joseph succeeded in diverting to the government treasury almost all the money in the country. This was, of course, of great advantage to the State.

In the second year the drought persisted as did the scarcity of food. But the Egyptians possessed no more precious metals to pay for the purchases of corn. Joseph was unconcerned and asked for the Egyptians' livestock, *horses and livestock, whether sheep or cattle, and . . . donkeys.*

In the third year the summer was again unrelenting and the Nile did not rise sufficiently. There was nothing left to eat. The starving Egyptians came to implore Joseph. They had no more money, and no more farm animals, but there still remained their land and their bodies. These they were willing to give. In exchange for *something to sow* Joseph agreed to accept them and their land and to distribute corn from the granaries.

When the fourth year came the situation was unchanged. Joseph offered the farmers, who were now reduced to the state of serfs, to provide them with grain on condition that at the harvest a fifth of it was to be given to Pharaoh.

The scribe who relates this story does not conceal his admiration for Joseph and his effective measures. It was a primitive period and the times were hard, but a tax of twenty per cent on income seems surprising, though it must be admitted that since those days we have progressed.

Jacob decides to adopt Joseph's two sons

For seventeen years Jacob, surrounded by his sons, had lived in the land of Goshen. He was now almost completely blind and feeling that death was near sent for his beloved son Joseph and made him promise under oath not to bury him in the land of Egypt; the son of Isaac, the grandson of Abraham, desired to lie in the cave of Machpelah, near Hebron, in company with 'his fathers'. Before he died he asked for Joseph's two sons, Manasseh and Ephraim, to be brought to him; he had decided to adopt them as his own. This provided the occasion for a curious ceremony which is summarily described in the Bible. For the occasion the two youths were placed in Jacob's lap (literally 'between the knees') while he sat on the edge of his bed. Jacob gave them the ritual kiss. Then Joseph took them from his father's arms and with his sons bowed to the ground before him. For the blessing they rose to their feet. Joseph was careful to place Manasseh, the elder, on Israel's right, and Ephraim, the younger, on his left. But the blind man crossed his hands, placing his right hand on the head of the younger and his left hand on the head of the firstborn, while pronouncing this imposed blessing:

> *May God in whose presence my fathers Abraham and Isaac walked,*
> *may God who has been my shepherd from my birth until this day,*
> *may the angel who has been my saviour from all harm, bless these boys,*
> *may my name live on in them, and the names of my fathers Abraham and Isaac.*
> *May they grow and increase on the earth.*

Joseph noticed the unusual position of Jacob's hands and this upset him. Of course, a blessing always remains valid, but one given with the right hand was reputed to be more efficacious. Joseph pointed this out to his father: *'Not like that, father! This one is the elder; put your right hand on his head.'* But his father refused: *'I know, my son, I know,'* he answered. And he went on to explain: *'He too shall become a people; he too shall be great. Yet his younger brother* [this obviously referred to the tribe of Ephraim] *shall be greater than he, and his descendants shall become a multitude of nations.'*

In fact, in the subsequent history of Israel the tribe of Ephraim was to play, as we shall have occasion to observe later on, a political, military and religious role of primary importance.

'Now I am about to die,' Jacob said to Joseph. *'But God will be with you and take you back to the country of your fathers'* (that is, the land of Canaan, modern Palestine). This was a prophecy of the Exodus from Egypt (which can be dated in about 1200, that is, something like four centuries after this prediction) and the settling of Yahweh's people in the Promised Land.

Jacob's oracles

Before breathing his last, the patriarch Jacob requested that his twelve sons should gather round his bed. There, in the presence of his sons he pronounced, not a series of blessings[21] but a series of oracles concerning the political and religious future of the twelve tribes which were to be formed at a later date around their twelve chieftains. Of each of these groups which was to be formed Jacob traces a rapid but characteristic psychological portrait, embellishing it sometimes with certain geographical features concerning the territories which several centuries later they would occupy.

According to the beliefs of those days the prophetic utterances of the dying man not only revealed, but

---

[21] The traditional title of this chapter of the Bible (*Jacob's blessings*) can well give a wrong impression. In fact among the twelve invocations uttered by the patriarch only two blessings are to be discerned — only Judah and Joseph are solemnly placed under Yahweh's protection. In what refers to the ten other brothers Jacob merely pronounces oracles, as is pointed out below.

conditioned the destiny of his twelve sons and in this way we are given, even at this point, the principal features of that part of the history of Israel concerning the particular territory of Canaan occupied by the twelve tribes. It seems quite probable that on his deathbed Jacob was granted a vision.

Nevertheless it must be pointed out that certain biblical commentators, including some of the most conservative, are inclined to think that the series of oracles are an instance of literary transposition. In their opinion, it is quite possible that the story-tellers, and even the scribes, felt obliged to put into Jacob's mouth matters observed several centuries after his death. But the reader must not conclude that this is a case of literary fraud or trickery. In the East there was never any hesitation in inserting an event of one period into the history of another if it was thought better to do so; this was a perfectly acceptable historical method. It remains for the modern critic of the texts, with all prudence and circumspection, to re-establish the chronological order.

'Gather round, sons of Jacob, and listen;
listen to Israel your father.'

At whatever date the reader decides to place the oracles of Jacob (either in about 1680, the time of his death, or in 1200–1000, the period when the twelve tribes of Israel settled in the land of Canaan) the interest of the information which they furnish about these Hebrew tribes is undeniable. Jacob speaks to us of his sons and of each of the tribes of Israel. Sometimes he apostrophizes them rather roughly, sometimes he uses language of great tenderness, according to the tribe of which he is speaking. These oracles form a series of moving passages which must be read in the Bible itself. They are not analysed in detail here, for it would seem that the study of the oracles of Jacob falls naturally into place at the period of the Hebrews' settling in Palestine with Joshua and his successors.

Embalming and funeral of Jacob

On various occasions already it has been pointed out that the Semites in general, and the Hebrews in particular, buried their dead without endeavouring in any way to preserve the corpses from the normal and natural disintegration and decay. And yet *the doctors embalmed Israel* we find in Genesis. This has caused some writers to assert that this detail of the biblical account is an obvious historical anachronism for, they say, at the time of the Pharaohs, doctors did not belong to the corporation of embalmers. But recent discoveries enable us to regard this intervention of the doctors as completely acceptable for we now know that a certain category of doctors was entitled to carry out this operation.

The few biblical scholars who have concerned themselves with this question seem scarcely to have arrived at the exact meaning of the sentence quoted above. The view put forward here is that Joseph took good care not to entrust the patriarch's body to the Egyptian experts in mummification, for this was an essentially religious operation. Thus the body of the dead person was rubbed with a sacred oil. The thorax and the abdomen were emptied of their contents which were replaced by a whole collection of different statuettes, representing the tutelary deities. At carefully specified places figurines of scarabs, hawks and so forth were inserted. Each bandage had in it a magic inscription enabling the dead person to identify himself to Osiris, thus providing him with the means of obtaining entry through the gates of the Beyond.

Despite his high office at Pharaoh's court, Joseph, we can be sure from many characteristic details, had remained entirely faithful to the religion of the patriarchs, his direct ancestors. He took good care not to profane his father's mortal remains by handing them over to idolatrous embalmers, who dabbled in occult powers and were the custodians of ritual formulas intended to open to the dead man the paradise of Osiris.

Jacob, the Bible informs us quite clearly, was not mummified in Egyptian fashion, but merely embalmed, just as is still done on occasion in modern civilization, by 'doctors'. These latter were only responsible for ensuring the preservation of the body which had to make the comparatively long journey through the desert of Zin, between the place where death took place (the land of Goshen) and the place determined for burial (Hebron).

It took them forty days, for embalming takes forty days to complete.

On this point the scribe is wrong: in Egypt mummification required seventy days' work (perhaps two days more or less). It is true that the preparation of Jacob's body was appreciably different from what was then current practice. In these circumstances the figure of forty days can be accepted, although it should perhaps be remembered that in the Old Testament, and occasionally in the New, the number forty is often used as the synonym for a long time (the forty years of the Exodus, Jesus' forty days' fast in the desert, etc.). At all events, the writer had no right to say that *embalming takes forty days to complete* in Egypt. This has raised objections from Egyptologists.

The Egyptians mourned him for seventy days.

Egyptologists have also objected that in Egypt the mourning period was exactly the same length as that required for the preparation of the mummy. As Jacob's

169

embalming took forty days the mourning period ought not to have exceeded this length of time. But the fact remains that Joseph, who had remained in his heart of hearts a Semite and a worshipper of Yahweh, had not in any way to comply with the ritual requirements and funeral customs of the Egyptians.

As a high official of the pharaoh, and the governor of the Delta, Joseph owed it to himself to give his father an imposing funeral. The whole family, therefore, *went up* to Hebron, *with chariots*. The scribe notes at this point, and with obvious satisfaction, that the procession was made up of *all Pharaoh's servants and the palace dignitaries . . .* [and] *all the dignitaries of the land of Egypt*. It almost seems surprising that Pharaoh did not go in person.

The funeral cortège arrived at Mamre in the oak grove where formerly Abraham had established his camp, and where Isaac and subsequently Jacob camped for some time. The organizers of the ceremony had arranged for *a long and solemn lamentation* to take place there. Then *Joseph observed three days' mourning for his father*. Finally the mortal remains of the patriarch Jacob were placed in the cave of Machpelah which had been bought from Ephron the Hittite by Abraham.

In this tomb, on stone benches, there lay already the bodies of Abraham and Sarah his wife, of Isaac and his wife Rebekah. And now, in his turn, Jacob was placed there. Subsequently, Leah was placed beside her husband, Jacob. Thus in the venerable crypt at Hebron — nowadays forming part of the Haram el-Khalil mosque — were laid the bodies of the three biblical patriarchs and their wives. Rachel is excepted, of course, for she had died during the journey of the clan from Haran, and Jacob was obliged to bury her at Ephrath by the side of the path (see page 99).

Joseph, who cannot be included among the patriarchs, was also brought back from Egypt. His body must have been embalmed, for it accompanied the Israelites on their wanderings across the Sinai wilderness during the forty years of the Exodus. His mummy finally found its resting place at Shechem, surrounded by the pastureland which Jacob before dying desired to bestow upon his son in addition to his legal share of the inheritance. A small white dome marks the traditional site of the tomb.

Further anxieties of Joseph's brothers

Jacob was dead. The ten brothers, who had been responsible for the evil deed perpetrated at Dan, were very worried. Had Joseph, they wondered, awaited the death of Jacob to take his personal vengeance on them in all tranquility? After all, it was perfectly legitimate for him to do so under the laws prevailing at the time. Without delay they sent in a petition to Joseph, reminding him of the patriarch's last words: *'You must say to Joseph: Oh forgive your brothers their crime and their sin and all the wrong they did you.'*

Obviously, they had not yet understood what could be accomplished by love of the neighbour and generosity of heart. On receiving their message Joseph was unable to hold back his tears. But the ten brothers were still exceedingly anxious. They asked to be received personally by him whom formerly they had sold as a slave; they desired to fall down before him with their heads in the dust, and in true eastern fashion they cried out to him, *'We present ourselves before you as your slaves.'* Joseph made haste to raise them up, reassuring them and speaking to them affectionately. *'The evil you planned to do me,'* he explained, *'has by God's design been turned to good, that he might bring about, as indeed he has, the deliverance of a numerous people.'*

In those merciless times when the law of retribution (the *lex talionis*) was applicable among the Semites, there had suddenly appeared, and for the first time in the Bible, the luminous notion of forgiveness of injuries. It was a new climate of charity in which the coming of better times was foreshadowed.

The Hyksos driven out of the Delta by the Egyptian national forces (1580 B.C.)

With the powerful protection of the vizier, a man of their own race, behind them, the group of Hebrews were able to achieve a comfortable life in the pleasant surroundings of the Wadi Tumilat. On the material level they were really well provided for. The flocks grazed on rich pasture-land, in meadows where the water from the canals drained from the Nile, and streams abounded. In the well-irrigated fields bordering the pasture the Israelites on occasion turned to horticulture and even to farming. Theirs was a pleasant life.

What was their religious position? As was pointed out above, in Egypt we no longer find recorded those imposing appearances of Yahweh with which the patriarchs were frequently honoured in former times in Canaan. Had the mysterious colloquies with Yahweh with which from time to time he encouraged his chosen ones come to an end?

It is true that the Israelites never forgot to render homage to the one God of Abraham; they continued to call upon him and invoke him. But by its very proximity the Egyptian religion was extremely dangerous. Its majestic temples towering in the nearby Delta, its splendid ceremonies taking place in its sanctuaries and especially its picturesque pantheon, appealing to the senses and the imagination, formed so many attractive elements calculated in course of time to seduce the followers of Yahweh whose theology offered them a holy and invisible God.

In addition, it must be admitted, the Israelites established in the land of Goshen increasingly lost interest in the Promised Land (Canaan, the future Palestine) where one day they were to settle. Life in the Tumilat valley was so pleasant, with the 'pans of meat' and 'bread to their heart's content', that it was difficult to see any reason for returning to Beersheba or even Hebron and the arduous life of wandering shepherds in the plains with the close cropped grass often burnt up by the sun. In this little corner of Egypt on the east side of the Delta they were living in a dreamland.

Now at the beginning of the sixteenth century, between the deaths of Jacob and Joseph, an Egyptian national dynasty, hitherto driven back to Thebes in the south, undertook a methodical war of liberation intended to achieve the permanent expulsion of the Hyksos from the valley of the Nile. A local Theban prince, Sequenenre I, of the seventeenth dynasty, began hostilities. The Egyptian armies won some outstanding victories, but also suffered heavy defeats. In the end, in about 1580, the pharaoh Ahmosis I, the embodiment of national resistance, managed to penetrate into the Delta and we find him taking the citadel of Avaris, the Hyksos capital. The fall of this military and political centre marks the downfall of the Hyksos empire. These invaders who had occupied Egyptian territory for more than two centuries were thrown back right into Canaan, and it is very probable that Amenhotep I (the son and successor of Ahmosis) pursued the remnant of the Hyksos army as far as Syria. He was concerned principally to guarantee the valley of the Nile against the offensive return of these invaders. To achieve this successive pharaohs led victorious expeditions as far as the banks of the Euphrates.

Genesis, which is not a political history of the ancient Near East, passes over these events in silence. At the very beginning of Exodus the writer confines himself to saying, *There came to power in Egypt a new king who knew nothing of Joseph.* We know the name of this new king; it was, as we have seen, Ahmosis I, a national hero, the conqueror of the Hyksos and the liberator of the country. With this new political régime in Egypt it was to be wondered whether Jacob's sons would enjoy so peaceful a life as hitherto.

The Israelites remain a further three and a half centuries in Egypt (1580–1225 B.C. – approximate dates)

1580: the Hyksos were driven out of the Delta by the Egyptian national army.

1225: the Israelites, of their own free will, left the land of Goshen: this was the Exodus under the leadership of Moses. Thus the Israelites remained about three and a half centuries after the departure of the Hyksos. What happened to the Israelites during this long period? The reader of the Bible might be tempted to think, somewhat too hastily, that directly after the defeat of the Hyksos Jacob's descendants experienced the persecution so horrifyingly described in one of the chapters of Exodus. In reality two successive and clearly defined periods must be distinguished: first a long period (two centuries and a half, perhaps even three centuries, 1580–1325/1275 B.C.) preceding the great persecution. The Israelites under fairly agreeable conditions continued their life as shepherds in the Wadi Tumilat region. This was followed by a much shorter period during which they suffered under the Egyptian policy which aimed at the systematic destruction of the Israelites remaining in Egypt.[22] These

[22] Did all the Israelites (the house of Jacob, Abraham's direct descendants) go down with the patriarch into Egypt? Modern scholarship is inclined to believe

174

are periods in the history of Israel which must now be examined in succession.

The period preceding the great persecution (1580–1325/1275)

Jacob was dead; seven years afterwards Joseph followed him to the grave. The former vizier of the Hyksos rulers does not seem to have been troubled by the new government of the pharaoh Ahmosis I, nor does it appear that he was asked to justify his collaboration with the occupying power. Of course, he lost no time in leaving his palace and as unobtrusively as possible rejoined the tents of his clan in the land of Goshen.

We have already seen the xenophobe character of the Egyptians, and so might expect to find that they treated very harshly the various groups which after the rapid departure of the Hyksos did not feel obliged to follow them. The Israelites were certainly not the only ones thus to stay where they were. It would be wrong to say that these foreigners were regarded with favour by the victorious Egyptians to whom they recalled memories of the hateful invaders, but, at the outset at least, they do not seem to have been seriously or systematically molested.

---

that some of the tribes of Israel never left the land of Canaan, and certain authors think only the clans of Joseph, Levi and Simeon went down to the Delta. The argument is a little far-fetched. On the other hand it might well be supposed that some clans, at the time of the defeat of the Hyksos, thought it prudent to follow them eastwards. This might in some measure account for the well-known inscription, dating from 1229, of the pharaoh Meneptah which speaks of the destruction of 'Israel' among the peoples defeated in Palestine. At this time, it must be emphasized, the house of Joseph was still in the land of Goshen. In fact, this whole question is extremely difficult to resolve. There are too many hypotheses and not enough facts. In such a case the historian must proceed with great prudence, since excavation may at any moment produce startling and more accurate information.

In this pastoral setting, which constituted a change, certainly, from the luxurious surroundings of his former palace, Joseph lived until the age of a hundred and ten — this age being regarded among the Egyptians as the ideal length for a full life. Thus he had the joy of being present at the birth of his children's children, the sons of Manasseh and Ephraim, whom he adopted as his heirs.

On his deathbed he performed a ceremony of a kind that we have already encountered: he *made Israel's sons* [that is, his brothers] *swear an oath, 'When God remembers you with kindness* [that is, when finally you set out for Canaan] *be sure to take my bones from here.'* For the time being, in fact, it was impossible to leave Egypt since at that period military operations were proceeding east of the Delta. Thus shortly after Joseph's death his body was embalmed. His coffin could not leave Egypt until three centuries after these events. The Israelites, led by Moses, then took with them Joseph's body during the forty years of marching and countermarching in the wilderness, before it was solemnly buried at Shechem when the Israelites entered the Promised Land (about 1200).

During this period in the Wadi Tumilat, the Hebrews continued to lead a relatively peaceful life. The proof of this is to be found in the fact that we find at this period an extraordinary growth in numbers. In this healthy fertile valley, Jacob's clan which numbered about seventy (not including, of course, the servants and slaves) increased to such an extent that, about three centuries afterwards — at the time of the Exodus — the Israelites could put in the field 60,000 men capable of bearing arms. On the basis of these figures it has been calculated that the total population of Israel amounted at this period to between two and a half millions and three millions.

This figure cannot be accepted, for at that rate the Israelites would have outnumbered all the other inhabitants of the valley of the Nile. This problem will be examined in greater detail in the chapter (in the next volume) dealing with the Exodus.

For the moment it should be noted that dwelling in the rich and fertile land of the Delta the tribe of Joseph became a people, the people of Israel. This could hardly have happened, at any rate so quickly, on the plains of Canaan where living conditions were far harder. Thus we can begin to understand the need for this sojourn in Egypt which enabled a small clan to show so rapid an increase in numbers.

This unexpected increase of the Israelite population did not pass unnoticed by the Egyptian authorities. The officials began to be worried. *'Look,'* they said, *'these people, the sons of Israel, have become so numerous and strong that they are a threat to us'* (this was an obvious exaggeration). Thereupon they began to spread alarming rumours of a tendentious character: *'We must be prudent and take steps against their increasing any further, or if war should break out, they might add to the number of our enemies. They might take arms against us.'*

What steps exactly were taken by the government is unknown. Were the Israelites taken for forced labour at this period? It is possible that they were from time to time, but it seems more probable that the officials of Ahmosis confined themselves to a stricter supervision of the activities and movements of the Israelites. Logically, a system of forced labour would not have enabled them to increase in numbers so rapidly. In any case the time of the great persecution was drawing near.

The period of the great persecution (1325/75–1225)

The following volume, devoted to Moses, deals with the

terrible ordeal undergone by Israel at the time of the nineteenth dynasty [23] whose monarchs transformed the Delta by their huge building enterprises, but a little must be said about it here. Rameses II, especially, was a great builder. On the ruins of Avaris, the former capital of the Hyksos, he built the city of Pi-Rameses. Everywhere colossal palaces and huge temples were put up. Between two campaigns Rameses was fond of resting for a time in this magnificent city which proclaimed his fame. The whole of the surrounding countryside was dotted with fortresses, warehouses and arsenals. He seems almost to have suffered from a building mania.

The map of the Delta (see p. 160) provides an explanation of the hard fate which was soon to overtake Israel: from the Wadi Tumilat (where the Israelites were still settled) to Pi-Rameses was scarcely a hundred miles. To ensure the rapid progress of these building operations the pharaoh's officials had already transported to the site a fairly numerous team of native workers, both from the Delta and even from the valley of the Nile. The rods of the supervisors on the labourers' backs made sure that they did not pause for a moment. The wall paintings in the tombs provide clear and highly coloured evidence of this.

Of course, it had been noticed that near at hand, in the frontier region bordering on the wilderness, was a fairly large number of asiatic shepherds who seemed to have no other care than watching their sheep and cultivating their vegetables. It was decided to commandeer these foreigners at once; no consideration was to be given to men whose detestable domination had been suffered for centuries during the occupation. It would form a golden opportunity for revenge on those whose ancestors – and

[23] The approximate dates are: 1320–1200. The names of the sovereigns were Rameses I, Rameses II, Seti, Meneptah – the last is regarded nowadays as the pharaoh at the time of the Exodus (about 1225).

Brick making; nothing has changed since the time when Pharoah forced Israel to make bricks.

here they remembered Joseph, the vizier of a Hyksos pharaoh — had not always shown themselves particularly gentle towards the Egyptian population.

Thus the Israelites, proud shepherds of the wilderness, quick to take offence, were sent off to the building sites where they were employed on the most arduous tasks — mixing the mud and sand, treading the clay to incorporate the chopped straw, moulding the bricks, carrying the materials, and all this under a relentless sun.

In the evening the unfortunate slaves, dropping with fatigue and sore from the blows that they had received, were taken back to their camps where their wives contrived somehow or other to prepare a frugal meal. They called on Yahweh. They often bemoaned their lot. One day their terrible affliction would come to an end as Joseph had foretold: *'I am about to die,'* he had said in the presence of his family, *'but God will be sure to remember you kindly and take you back from this country to the land that he promised on oath to Abraham, Isaac and Jacob.'* And so they waited, though time did not seem to bring the slightest change in the situation.

There was a high death rate and a considerable decrease in the number of births. Moreover, for some time past, the Egyptians had decided that all the male children of the Israelites should be thrown into the Nile at birth. And how many of the Israelites succumbed daily under the lash of the slave drivers? How did they hope ever to escape from their terrible predicament?

'A papyrus basket, coated with bitumen and pitch' (Exod. 2: 3)

One morning a young Egyptian princess with the girls attending her went down to bathe in the river. And there in the reeds near the bank she saw floating on the water a small papyrus basket. Quite naturally she hastened to open the mysterious package; it contained a young Israelite only a few months old. It was easy to see what had happened: a mother, belonging to a group of Asiatic shepherds reduced to slavery, had been unable to resign herself to giving up her new-born child to Pharaoh's executioners. For a time she had managed to conceal its existence, but she knew that she could not do so for long. And so the unfortunate woman decided to place the child in the basket and entrust it to the waters of the Nile. On the spot the princess made up her mind to adopt the foundling. She called him Moses and brought him up at the royal court.

Some decades later Moses, the Hebrew, received from Yahweh in person the mission of bringing out of Egypt the Chosen People and bringing back the house of Israel to the Promised Land. At that time there appeared in all its splendour, in all its strength, the brilliant personality of Moses, the man of God, the inspired prophet, the religious chief, the leader of men and the inspired lawgiver.

EPILOGUE

The Hebrew patriarchs at the bar of history

This concludes the adventures of the three patriarchs Abraham, Isaac and Jacob, the pioneers of monotheism, the first founders of that spiritual order on which was established the moral bases of western civilization.

Before closing the Book of Genesis[1] it may be well to consider, still as an historian, a final question: what, on

[1] It should be borne in mind that Genesis is made up of two separate parts: 1. What some commentators call, very rightly indeed, 'the prehistory of humanity' (chapters 1–11); 2. the prehistory of the people of Israel. In this book, as in the first volume of the series (Abraham) the historical commentary has of set purpose been confined to this second part concerning the three patriarchs, God's chosen ones.

a last analysis, is the documentary value of this story of the patriarchs? To give an honest answer to this question we must consider separately what exactly are the elements of the problem to be solved. Consequently our first inquiry concerns the precise literary category to which Genesis belongs. We then go on to inquire whether according to modern historical criteria the actual text goes back to a date that is sufficiently ancient for it to be taken seriously. Thirdly and lastly, we shall have to see whether the various historical matters referred to in the narrative show evidence of the authenticity required by the historian.

To what literary category does Genesis belong?

To be in a position to furnish a critical judgement on a book of history it is important to know first of all in what circumstances it was composed, for what readers it was intended, in what period it was published. Is it to be classified as 'memoirs' or among works of learning. Is it a biography or the history of a nation? What is the author's avowed or hidden objective? The answers to these questions will enable us to place the work with which we are concerned in the literary category to which it strictly belongs. With this in mind we can investigate to what category of historical writing Genesis belongs.

Some have called it a 'saga' or 'epic', others have called it a kind of 'lyrical epic'. And indeed Genesis is a sort of epic, as will be shown.

What is an epic?

The epic is the primitive form of history as it emerges in some civilizations that are not primitive but archaic. At that time, man, beginning to free himself from the grasp of material concerns, was endeavouring to recall, and to establish, the past of his own human group.

We are nowadays fairly well informed about the mechanism which caused this literary form to originate; it appears to have been subject, in places and periods far removed from each other, to almost identical laws – the same process of formation, the same evolutionary tempo, the same mishaps and, finally, its crystallization into the form in which it has come down to us.

Consider an example that is well known, at least in its principal features: the Iliad, the epic attributed to Homer which celebrates the exploits of the Achaean warriors in ancient Greece who had led a punitive expedition against Troy on the Asiatic coast of what is now known as the Dardanelles.

Modern scholarship has shown that Homer, the blind bard, and author of this poem, probably never existed. Seven cities contended for the honour of being his birthplace; it is very possible that in each of these seven cities a blind bard composed and recited, to the accompaniment of a harp (the instrument used merely to provide a kind of musical background), some of the extraordinary adventures of the great Achaean leaders: of Agamemnon, king of Argos, commander of the Greek host that went to Troy; of Menelaus, the two Ajax, Ulysses and Achilles, and many another besides. Nowadays we know that the Iliad (like its younger sister the Odyssey) must be regarded as a collective work, put together in the course of several centuries by wandering harp-playing poets who went from city to city, from island to island, with their 'songs', to entertain the popular audiences eager for historical recitals.

The Trojan war took place in about the twelfth century B.C. For hundreds of years the 'Homeric' epics developed in various centres. Bards recounted the prowess of the heroes of Tiryns, Mycenae, Sparta, Ithaca and other centres of Argolis on the islands. The events recounted were several centuries old but the memory of them was preserved by oral tradition from one generation to another. Of course, as is obvious, from time to time a new picturesque feature was inserted, or an outstanding detail, to show off more effectively some person, scene or event.

Now in about 600 B.C. a certain Pisistratus seized Athens, and, being a man of very great energy, he decided to gather together all these rhapsodies designated by the term 'homeric' which were recited or chanted in the continental or insular regions of Greece in Europe or Greece in Asia. Thus the new ruler ordered an anthology to be compiled in which were collected the twenty-four poems of the Achaean epic. The Iliad, as we now know it, was born.

Modern Hellenists have no difficulty in showing that this work was made up of very different elements. One passage is written in the Ionian dialect, another in the Doric. Vocabulary and syntax differ from one piece to another and the images used show that the poets belonged to different regions and successive periods. That is how the Iliad appears when subjected to rigorous examination by the philologists.

It was pointed out above that the epic is history as it could be conceived by a dawning civilization. What therefore is to be the attitude of the modern historian, who is extremely exacting about the objective reality of recorded events, when faced with this composite work? In this epic poem in which the statements, some of them contradictory, are often difficult to confirm or harmonize, how can the scientific historian glean evidence that can be used for a systematic reconstruction of the past?

At the end of the last century specialists in the history of ancient Greece 'believed in the Iliad'. It is not surprising therefore that at that period the German archaeologist Heinrich Schlieman carried out excavations on the site of ancient Troy, the former capital of King Priam, taking as his guide the indications to be found in Homer. He brought to light impressive treasures, though at the same time he perpetrated some of the worst of historical blunders.

Does that mean that nowadays Hellenists working on the sites in Greece and the coasts of Asia Minor leave the indications to be found in Homer entirely out of account? By no means. Many passages of the Iliad have provided very interesting clues. It gives for instance details of considerable interest about Achaean arms, customs and the tactics of the warriors of this period and the nautical knowledge of the Greeks of the thirteenth century B.C. Of course, we are sometimes obliged to correct certain details; on occasion the authors are guilty of anachronisms; the findings of modern excavations make considerable correction necessary. But the general effect of the narrative is one of undeniable authenticity.

These few observations show how the use of these basic elements reveals hitherto unsuspected possibilities for historical research. The historical form of the epic enables us to obtain information whose authenticity is often confirmed by the findings of archaeology. The people depicted are real; their general behaviour is often in close agreement with the data furnished by archaeology or philology. Of course, bearing in mind the tendency of the bards to amplify their narratives, and taking into account the inevitable anachronisms in their matter, we are obliged now and then to reduce some of the episodes to their proper proportions. It is obviously not difficult to make due allowance for a certain verbal inflation or exaggeration which is characteristic of this epic literature.

Similarly, it could be shown that the Chanson de

Roland, under the influence of the troubadours, developed in the same way as the Iliad; and the same method could be applied to examination of the origin and development of other epics such as the Niebelungen of the northern countries or the Saga of Erik the Red, the fearless navigator who arrived on the coast of North America several centuries before Christopher Columbus.

History originated, we see, in the form of the epic. It appeared, developed and became fixed almost under the same conditions, whatever the young and dynamic civilization which gave it birth. Here and there we find it with the same qualities and the same defects. With this in mind we can return to Genesis.

Genesis: the epic character of its origins

We must first investigate the date of the text. That part of the Bible which we call Genesis was written down, in the form that we have it, during the sixth century B.C. when the elite of the Israelites, deported by Nebuchadnezzar to central Mesopotamia (this was the Babylonian Exile, 586–538) were in a position to return to Jerusalem. At that time the facts recorded in the narrative (namely the adventures of the patriarchs, 1850–1600) went back, therefore, upwards of a thousand years.

But the sixth-century scribe was using historical materials which had already been written down at the time of David and Solomon, that is, round about the year 1000 B.C. Before that date the historical traditions in question had been preserved solely in oral form. This is not so disquieting a statement as may at first sight appear: these religious narratives were preserved intact and with great devotion by the nomad Hebrew shepherds and then by the Israelites who had settled in the Promised Land. Special care was taken not to change a word of these sacred narratives. Even nowadays ethnologists are sometimes astonished at the interminable genealogies of the chieftains of Arab tribes which are transmitted orally without a mistake. Until the time of Jesus, and even for some time afterwards, the teaching of the rabbis was always oral; the disciples, although able to write, did not take the slightest note, and they could know by heart the whole of the Hebrew books of the Bible and recite them in their entirety. When Islam was first preached and for centuries afterwards the Koran was transmitted in oral form.

Thus just as with the Iliad and other epics of later date, in the case of Genesis we must admit that historical facts were faithfully transmitted by oral tradition. This indeed is one of the characteristics of the epic cycles.

As in all other forms of the epic, in the narrative of Genesis there can be discerned the undeniable presence of several traditions which differ in spirit, vocabulary and images. Fortunately the sixth-century writer who produced the definitive text took care not to rewrite these traditions to make a synthesis. He confined himself to putting them together, one after the other, without concerning himself with their sometimes contradictory statements. [2]

Philologists have succeeded in distinguishing the constituent elements. They have been able to isolate in the text the presence of several 'cycles' (some commentators prefer the term 'traditions'). Thus we have the Yahwistic cycle (designated in abbreviation by the letter J) in which God is called Yahweh. The narrator here

[2] A typical example is to be found in chapters 6 and 7, each of which in its own way relates the material cause of the Flood: the rising of the waters from below, flooding (6: 17), torrential rain. In 6: 19–20 Noah takes into the ark a pair of *all living creatures, from all flesh; 'they must be a male and a female'* says Yahweh. A few lines further down, 7: 2, Yahweh orders that seven of each kind of *clean animals* and only two of the *unclean* be taken in. There is a further contradiction: according to 7: 24 it says that the deluge lasted forty days and forty nights, but in 7: 24 it says that the waters rose on earth for a hundred and fifty days. The duality of the traditions followed by the final writer explains these variations.

makes use of a colourful vivid style, full of life. The Elohistic cycle (E) is easily recognizable from the fact that God is called 'Elohim. In addition, the text of Genesis was influenced, but to a lesser degree, by the Priestly cycle (P) and also by another cycle, the Deuteronomist (D). There are therefore four principal traditions used in the final shaping of the narrative.

We are a long way, it must be admitted, from the old idea, no longer held nowadays, of the 'inspired' writer taking it all down at God's dictation. But we are far nearer to the classic form of all epic literature.

Genesis: its distinctly epic character

Of course it could be objected that Genesis differs from western epics because the latter are essentially martial in inspiration (the Trojan war, the battle of Roncevaux and so on), while the adventures of the Hebrew patriarchs related in Genesis are almost solely concerned with religious matters. The argument cannot be sustained. Although the Aryan may take pleasure in the detailed accounts of great battles, and the Semite may prefer the relation in narrative form of the various stages of his spiritual evolution, in both instances the subject matter remains fundamentally *national*: it is concerned with a hero of whom one is proud to be the descendant or at least the fellow-countryman. That is a characteristic feature of all epics.

In addition, in the epic — whether Homeric, Hebrew or Carolingian — both the bard and his audience were interested only in the outstanding person portrayed. For the modern historian far too many material details remain obscure. The political circumstances of the period are mentioned with regrettable brevity. All the contemporaries of these recitals were, of course, familiar with the general pattern of daily life and its joys and sorrows. What reason was there, then, to mention it? Only occasionally did the narrator allow himself, almost by accident it seemed, to let drop certain remarks, certain observations, which for the historian in modern times are of enormous interest. The epic, whatever the country of its origin, provided far more information about the psychology of the heroes — Abraham, Ulysses, Roland, Siegfried, Erik — than on the general background to their experiences. There can be no question of expecting the narrator of this primitive form of history, which the epic is, to provide us with information with the same concern for detail, the same preoccupations, as the modern archivist.

Finally, the epic character of Genesis must be emphasized once more. In some places, in certain scenes, obvious exaggerations can be discerned. Later on, attention will be drawn to some of these exaggerations, both in the language used and the images employed, which are obviously intended to enhance the reputation of the national hero. All this can be explained by the state of mind and the profound tendencies of the period, and especially by the audiences which demanded marvels of all sorts. In any case, these makers of primitive history did their best from the documentary point of view. The specialist who is to some extent acquainted with their civilization cannot expect more of them.

That from the literary point of view the successive writers of Genesis succeeded in producing a masterpiece is undeniable, but this is outside our object.

Genesis and the historian

Despite the errors and anachronisms to be found on occasion in the Iliad, we can be certain that the Trojan War really took place. Indeed, without the Iliad we should not know of this extraordinary expedition. The site of Troy could have been excavated and it could have furnished its treasures but without revealing the secret of its history. We can be grateful to the bards.

Despite obvious exaggerations, and the extravagant images to be found from time to time in the Chanson de Roland, the attack and destruction of Charlemagne's rearguard at Roncevaux remain authentic historical facts, at least as a whole.

Despite certain matters that the scientist finds difficult to accept the text of Genesis gives every appearance of an authentic witness, the reflection of an epic civilization whose reality cannot be denied. Nowadays the results of excavations and the discovery of 'written documents' in Egypt and Mesopotamia, enables the critical method to be used in the study of the texts. The respect due to the Bible in no way requires that we should place our intelligence under a bushel.

In conclusion: Genesis, a work of archaic character, is of considerable value for the ancient history of the Near East, and, by definition, without equal for all that concerns the history of the people of God. But we cannot confine ourselves to these considerations of Genesis as epic literature. Two further questions remain to be asked:

1. Did the sixth-century scribe, the final editor of the sacred text, use *ancient* documents for his work?

2. Are these documents authentic?[3]

Antiquity of the historical materials utilized by the the writer of Genesis (sixth century)

If a modern archivist were to ask us to show him a document contemporary with Abraham, Isaac and Jacob, or

[3] The reader who desires to pursue this entrancing but delicate inquiry further can consult to good purpose several works which have dealt with this matter with the tact and historical objectivity required. There is, first and foremost, the work of Daniel Rops, *What is the Bible?* (London and New York, 1958). The explanations given below have been based on the general plan and very objective commentary furnished by Fr de Vaux in his 'Introduction to the Pentateuch' at the beginning of the *Jerusalem Bible*.

even with Joseph, to provide scientific proof of the existence of the biblical patriarchs, we should be very embarrassed to find an answer. Not one Mesopotamian brick, not one roll of papyrus, not a single Canaanite inscription, mentions this clan of shepherds. The explanation, of course, is simple: the tiny group of wandering shepherds, obscure and unobtrusive as they were, whom we have followed over the steppe and in the wilderness, obviously had no reason to arouse the interest or provoke the attention of the annalists working for the two great powers of the period, the pharaohs of the valley of the Nile and the monarchs of Mesopotamia. These two political blocs had, we may be sure, other things to do than to establish the historical archives of this Semitic group. Nor should anything of this kind be expected of the Hebrew shepherds themselves; they were probably illiterate and certainly not concerned with the careful collection of documents for the purpose of giving complete satisfaction in the remote future to the learned men of the twentieth century A.D. There is therefore no 'material' proof. How indeed could there be since from 1850 (the time of Abraham) down to the year 1000 (the approximate date when Genesis *began* to be written down) the lyrico-epic tradition was handed down solely by word of mouth.

It was transmitted orally. In the preceding pages mention has been made of the extraordinary memories of people in the East. And in the West, also, similar feats are to be found. The present writer knows a priest of the diocese of Paris who can recite, word for word, the whole of the Pentateuch, and in Greek. There is no reason for surprise, then, if among us in the West the poems known under the name of Homer, before being written down in Athens by Pisistratus, were preserved for centuries by the harp-playing bards. For hundreds of years also the strophes of the epic of Roland at Roncevaux survived solely in the form in which they were sung until they assumed their definitive form from the pen of a diligent and informed copyist. No one nowadays would throw doubt on the Odyssey or the Song of Roland, and anyone who did so would have to contend with the arguments of the learned in these matters.

In fact, the same process is at work everywhere in the production of an epic cycle; the long 'oral' period of the story-tellers or bards necessarily precedes the definitive written form. The Book of Genesis passed through the same literary stages as the epics of Greece or of the West and the Scandinavian sagas. Thus we have every right to conclude, both by direct observation and by analogy, that Genesis is made up of very ancient elements. Just as Pisistratus in sixth-century Athens did not himself compose the Iliad, neither did the anonymous scribe of this same sixth century himself write Genesis. Philologists have proved that these two compositions, the Iliad and Genesis – and the same proof could be adduced for the other national epics – were conditioned by various elements of different origins placed side by side, elements which date back to the remote period of the story-tellers. Thus it seems certain that the materials utilized were very ancient. But are these materials authentic?

Authenticity of the historical materials utilized by the writer of Genesis

We can now endeavour to discover whether the pastoral civilization of the Hebrews, as it is shown to us in Genesis, is in contradiction with the findings of the archaeologists or the orientalists.

Geography

Genesis gives an accurate description of the country.

The principal route followed by Abraham and his sons hardly deviates from the watershed of the different mountain ranges by which they passed. The pasturelands and the oases (of which, as a city-dweller, the sixth-century scribe could have no personal experience) are correctly sited. The various types of steppe, whether grassy or semi-wilderness, as they are described bear the stamp of truth. There are of course anachronisms, as in all epic literature, on the subject of certain cities and peoples. But most of the urban centres mentioned were already in existence at the time of the patriarchs. Taken as a whole, therefore, Genesis is in agreement with the results of archaeological excavation.

History

Abraham left Ur: this departure coincided with a general movement of populations in the middle of the nineteenth century B.C. in lower Mesopotamia. As is made clear by Genesis the fortified cities of the future Palestine were occupied by the Canaanites, who were polytheists. The religion attributed to them by the Bible is exactly the same as that which has recently been discovered by the archaeologists. Joseph's adventure (between about 1650 and 1600) occurred under the military occupation of the Hyksos in the Egyptian Delta. Generally speaking there is agreement with the findings of archaeology.

Ethnology

The descriptions furnished by Genesis about the Hebrew clan proves to us that they belonged to the category of donkey-riding nomads, and were raisers of smaller livestock. In addition they were Arameans whose centre was at Haran in the valley of the Upper Euphrates. At Haran Abraham stayed for some time. Isaac married an Aramean woman from Haran (Rebekah) and his son two Arameans women from the same place (Leah, Rachel). All these nomads were peace-loving people; unlike the camel-riding nomads they never took part in raids. They detested the use of arms. In general all these characteristics agree with the findings of the archaeologists and orientalists.

Legislation

In the legislation an obvious connection can be discerned between the very ancient Mesopotamian codes (codes of Eshunna and Lipit-ishtar) and the unwritten law customarily applied by the Hebrew patriarchs. In the two books devoted to the ancestors of the people of Israel I have been careful to emphasize on several occasions the borrowings effected by the chieftains of the clan from Sumerian legislation (buying of land, adoption rites etc.). They were very ancient customs, carefully preserved by Abraham, his son and his grandson.

Orientalists entirely agree on this point.

Nomenclature

Certain proper names of the patriarchal period have been discovered on Mesopotamian tablets which constituted the royal library; these are of very early date. Abraham appears on a Babylonian tablet of the sixteenth century. The name Jacob is to be found on several occasions in a text of Mari (on the Upper Euphrates) of the eighteenth century B.C. (in the form which also occurs in the list of the Pharaoh Thutmosis, ya'qob-'El; this is of the fifteenth century); a Hyksos chief is called Ya 'qob-har. On the site at Mari have also been discovered the names of Levi and Simeon. Thus the names mentioned by Genesis agree in general with the results of archaeological excavations.

Although from the historian's critical examination the

Bible emerges endowed with a new and unquestioned prestige, it would be hazardous to state that the sacred text has not on occasion its weak points. These cannot be imputed to its originator but solely to the human agent who produced it. As Mgr Weber, bishop of Strasbourg, pertinently remarks, 'the Bible is a divine book, but it is not a book which dropped readymade from heaven'. Its sacred character and its title of 'holy' belong to it because for the first time since the beginning of man, and in terms which have never been equalled, it relates for us the sublime dialogue which, over thousands of years, was exchanged between God and man.

SELECT BIBLIOGRAPHY

The Jerusalem Bible; Darton, Longman & Todd (London), Doubleday and Company Inc. (New York)

General Books

A Catholic Commentary on Holy Scripture; Nelson (London)

Peake's Commentary on the Bible (Revised Edition); Nelson (London)

L. H. Grollenburg, *O. P.: Atlas of the Bible;* Nelson (London)

R. de Vaux, *O. P.: Ancient Israel;* Darton, Longman & Todd (London), McGraw-Hill Book Company (New York)

J. L. McKenzie, *S. J.: Dictionary of the Bible;* Chapman (London), The Bruce Publishing Co. (Milwaukee)

J. Bright: *A History of Israel;* S. C. M. Press (London), Westminster Press (Philadelphia)

T. Maertens: *Bible Themes;* Darton, Longman & Todd (London), Fides Publishing Inc. (Indiana)

C. Charlier: *The Christian Approach to the Bible;* Sands Publishers (Glasgow)

Books About Genesis

J. Blenkinsopp: *From Adam to Abraham;* Darton, Longman & Todd (London), Paulist Press (New York)

G. von Rad: *Genesis;* S. C. M. Press (London), Westminster Press (Philadelphia)

Select Bibliography

J. Rhymer: *The Beginnings of a People;* Sheed & Ward
(London), Pflaum Press (Dayton, Ohio)

A. Richardson: *Genesis;* S. C. M. Press (London), the
Macmillan Company (New York)

B. Vawter: *A Path through Genesis;* Sheed & Ward
(London)

INDEX OF NAMES

INDEX OF PLACES

Index of Places

Nihil obstat: John M. T. Barton, S.T.D., L.S.S., Censor.
Imprimatur: Patrick Casey V.G.
Westminster, 9 August 1968.